Imaginary Dances

More Themes for Children Dancing

Imaginary Dances

More Themes for Children Dancing

Rosa Shreeves

Dance Books • Alton

First published in 1998

This edition published in 2010 by
Dance Books Ltd
The Old Bakery, 4 Lenten Street
Alton, Hampshire GU34 1HG

© 2010 Rosa Shreeves

ISBN 978-1-85273-144-1

A CIP catalogue record for this book is available
from
the British Library

Illustrations by Rosa Shreeves
with Mike Komarnyckyj and Ray Burrows (page 13)
Photographs by Rosa Shreeves

Dedication

To My Mother
Full Circle

Acknowledgements

Jay Burton and her class at Hogarth Junior School, London W4
Ann Davies (Curriculum Adviser for Dance, Northants)
Antonia Guerrero (Dancer, Mexico City)
Jodi Page-Clark and the Holton Lee Community, Dorset
Will Menter (Musician/Composer)
Eric Needham (Education Consultant)
Roger North (Composer)
Bosco Oliveira (Percussionist)
Terry Cooper and Jennifer Roth (Directors of Spectrum Centre for Humanistic and Integrative Therapy, London)

and to:
all the children, young people and adults with whom I have worked and who over the years have given me so much stimulation, affirmation and delight in my dance.

Contents

Introduction

This book is about imaginary dances which in the writing of them, develop a logic and flow of their own (just as actual dances do); the creative nature of the writing reflecting the creative process in dance making. The ideas originate from a belief in the importance of the imaginative life of the child and stem from many years experience of both performing and creating similar dances with children and young people.

Imaginary Dances is a companion volume to *Children Dancing*, for teachers wanting to move from the basics into more depth, and into detailed ideas about putting dance scenarios into practice. While recognizing the diversity of aims in movement teaching, the emphasis in this book is on making and shaping dances. Children love to work towards a performance as long as the imaginative aspect of the work is kept alive by encouraging their creativity within a clear framework throughout the process. The ideas can gradually be refined over a number of weeks. Of course only *parts* of the different scenarios can always be selected.

The book can be used prescriptively by teachers, or as a starting point for their own creativity. It provides for those wanting clear guidance, as well as those with their own ideas who wish to increase their skills and range of possibilities.

Each chapter is based on a particular topic or project (nine in all). These are very varied and give opportunity for a wide range of dance and related experiences. Movement material is selected from a variety of imaginative starting points and then specific ways to form a dance or choreography are suggested. The dances are intended as a stimulus for making these or similar dances.

The imaginary dances can be thought of as examples of creative process; how one idea leads to another and how there are many possible ways of creating a dance – a process of continuous transformation between imagination, words and movement and between the text and the reader. The form and content of each dance is deliberately different but the style of writing throughout is intended to convey a sense of movement. Each chapter is self contained, and can be taken in any order according to your interests and circumstances. Ideas from one chapter might well be transposed onto another by the more experienced teacher.

A highly visual book, it stands as a resource on its own, but also more than covers the requirements of the National Curriculum*. Movement content is put into meaningful contexts.

The book is for Primary teachers and children but will be useful to a wide range of people: those involved with young people, with special needs groups, with the community and with performance.

Some chapters begin with a *Visualization* where the children are encouraged to use their imaginations, to create a 'mind picture' as an inner preparation for action and a transition time before movement. Visualizations could be read out as they stand, by suggesting that everyone sits comfortably still, perhaps with their eyes closed. Or the visualizations could be used as a basis for the teacher's own creative imagery.

For clarity of communication, very specific ways for the children to move have been suggested in *Making Movement* sections, but of course these are not immutable. When you have chosen a topic, read the dance ideas through slowly, giving yourself time to feel and imagine the movement described. Allow your own imagination and ideas to be stirred.

Evocative language and imagery are intended to suggest movement ideas to both teachers *and* children.

Extracts from the book itself might be read or shown to the children and their responses and suggestions encouraged. Once the movement ideas have been chosen and introduced, allow plenty of time for the movement flow and logic to appear.

The degree of development possible will obviously depend on the age and maturity of the participants involved. Part of a topic can always be selected. *Implicit is the notion that the dance is a collaborative process between the children, the teacher and the material.*

"..it is from your observation and theirs that the dance material progresses".**

It is helpful to think of movement itself as a language, which gradually increases in depth, skill and quality. In the end it is the combination of movement, imagination and each child's personal connection to the ideas which will make the dance a satisfying, learning experience.

"Only through focusing on the physical sensation and feeling in their movement and their bodies do children achieve that state of personal involvement from which creativity springs and which is beautiful to observe." **

Visual art forms and creating music with voice or percussion instruments, are frequently interwoven into the dance ideas and references are made to other aspects of the curriculum in the section, *Related Activities*. Collaborations with a music department are useful, particularly where large groups can be subdivided for the different activities.

The emphasis throughout the book is on fostering the interconnections between the body, mind and imagination and encouraging skills for the clear and formulated expression of ideas through movement. The underlying belief is in the importance of integrative movement and dance in education and personal development.
Through dance and all the arts we can make profound connections with ourselves and develop deeper and more satisfying contact and communication with others.

* The National Curriculum requirements on page 108 can be used as a minimal checklist for your observations. Specific dances from other traditions are not included in this book. There are also some links with the Art, Music and History (Aztec) N.C. See page 110.

** *Children Dancing* (Ward Lock Educational, 3rd edition, 1994) gives many explicit, useful examples of how to encourage creative dance, the nature of warm ups, movement development and the use of accompaniment. Less experienced teachers will find that the ideas in *Children Dancing* (Part 1) will support their basic understanding of dance teaching methods and principles not reiterated in this book.

R. O. Shreeves.

ANIMALS

In many ancient cultures people believe that they first learnt to dance from the animals and that certain animals have magical powers. In imitating their movements and feeling the essence of the animal through the dance you can learn from their particular qualities. The movements themselves will help define you and strengthen you. In North American Indian tradition there are many dance rituals associated with nature. Certain animals will carry special "medicine" for you and when called upon will bring you their wisdom and power.

The animal cards used in this chapter are a fun way to enter into this idea. You do not predetermine which animal will come to you but accept whichever one does and dance your identification with it.

Making the cards

Here, for simplicity, only four animals have been chosen.

DEER

FROG

LION

SNAKE

The cards can be the size of ordinary playing cards.

They can either be drawn, traced from the examples provided (on the next page) or the animal word itself printed on a card.

Make enough for one per child, e.g. for 32 children: 8 deer, 8 frogs, 8 lions and 8 snakes.

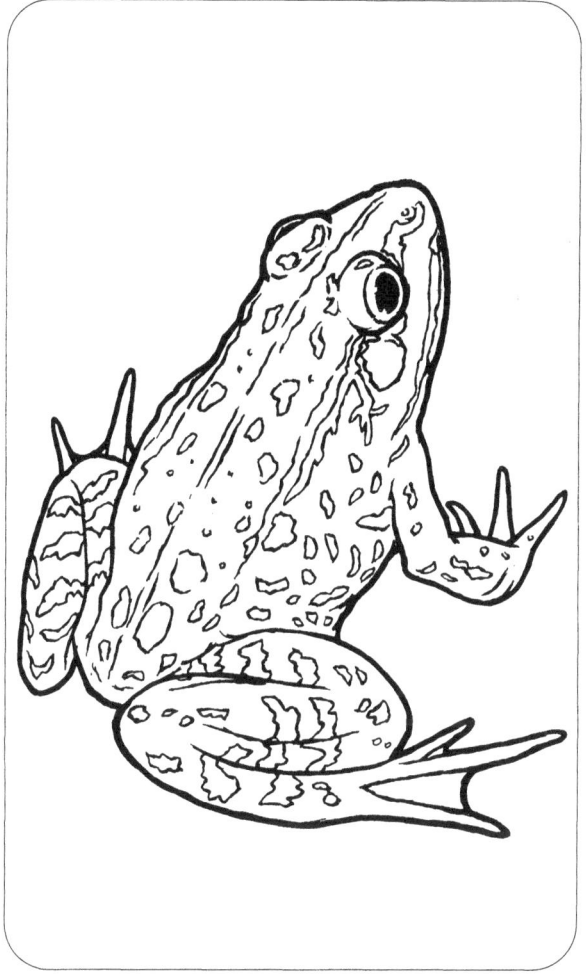

1. Calling upon the animal

All the cards are put face down on a brightly coloured cloth in the centre of the room. Everyone *sits quietly* around the cloth waiting for the choosing ceremony to begin. They can be thinking what help they would like from the animals – perhaps they have a problem that needs a solution, or a wish to be fulfilled or they may just be open and receptive to whatever ideas will emerge from the animals and the dance.

Choosing a card
To the gentle sound of flute music, each person walks quietly and meditatively one at a time to the centre of the room, chooses a card and returns to their place.

Here they turn the card over and spend a few minutes looking at the animal picture (or word) and identifying for themselves any associative movements, ideas and qualities of the animal that has 'chosen' them.

They then return the cards to the centre, go back to their place and take up a position, a body shape to represent their animal.

(At this point the cards can be quickly folded into the cloth and left there or removed from the movement space.)

2. Finding your animal tribe

The aim here is to gather into four groups:

DEER, FROGS, LIONS AND SNAKES.

At a given signal, all the animals simultaneously begin to travel about the room:

TROTTING LIGHTLY,   LEAPING,   PROWLING,   OR   UNDULATING,

showing the movements of deer, frog, lion and snake.

As soon as the children encounter another of their kind they stay near them in their animal shape until all four groups have gathered. You then have four still 'pictures' of the four animals.

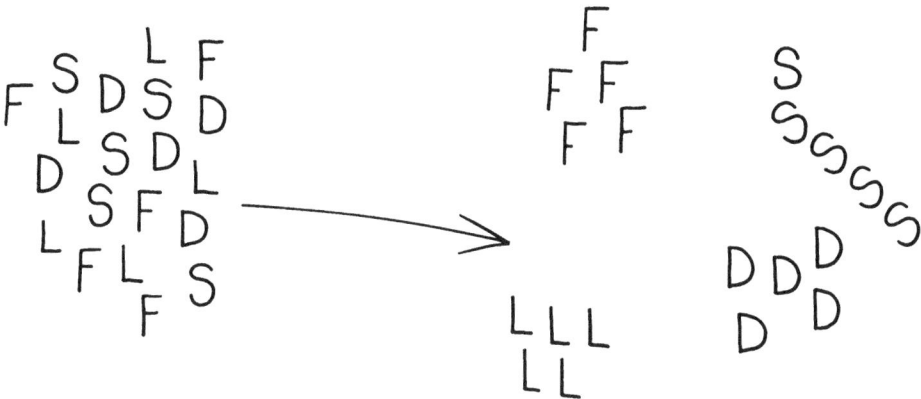

Usually this works really well after a bit of initial chaos. An alternative version is to call out the name of one of the animals e.g. 'FROGS' and at a signal all the frogs move and gather together into a still group, then the next animal is called out and moves, etc.

3. Making the movement of each animal

Initially every child can join in all the animal movements i.e. a whole class practice of each animal. After another practice period give an opportunity for each animal group to practise separately and then show their ideas while the others sit and watch. (The different groups might well practise at the same time.)

Twisting around (page 20)

DEER

Visualization

Imagine a forest –
a quiet deep wood –
with sun dappled shade –
where the deer are moving –
hardly seen –
hardly heard –
amongst the trees –

Movement

As Deer, practise moving gently, softly,
WALKING AND STOPPING
TURNING THE HEAD TO one side, then the other
TROTTING phrases – light running
PAWING the ground
GALLOPING (as when the herd is alerted)
SHIVERING your skin (to repel insects – all grazing animals do this)

Repeat each phrase lots of times, improving for example the clarity of the action and the use of the whole body. Then make combinations of the above actions. e.g. eight gallops forward, stop, two turns of the head, a shiver and a trotting turn.

Make the phrases rhythmic – use repetition – vary the travelling directions. Then choose several contrasting phrases and all learn to do them in unison. It could be like a little story. Make the FLOOR PATTERN clear.

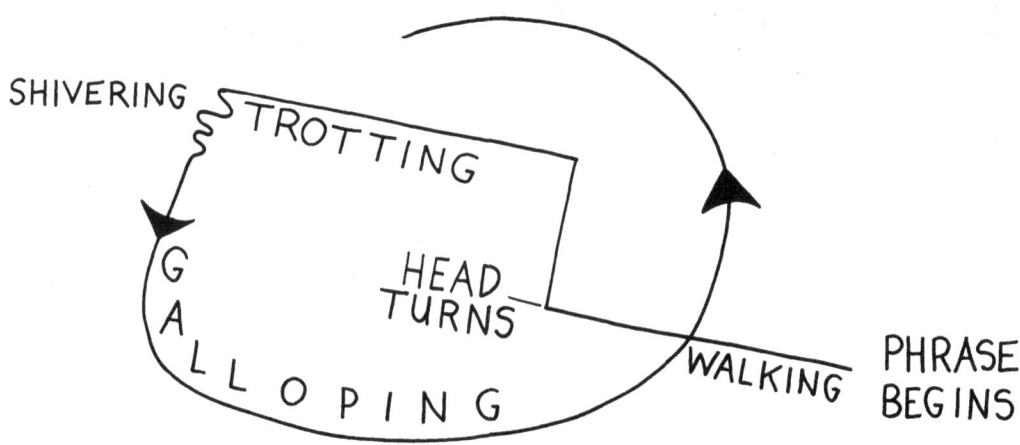

FROGS

Organize the frogs in a circle.

Visualization
Imagine you are round a pond – crouching down – in frog crouches.

Movement

Then.................... OOPS.............

A frog JUMPS in the air and lands somewhere in the circle, breathing in and

out with big swelling breaths.

Then another frog jumps in, then another – all jumping off two feet –

stretching up into the air, until all the frogs are jumping and pausing, still as

frog statues.

TRY TO JUMP

INTO THE SPACE

ANOTHER FROG

HAS JUST

LEFT

Then jump back to the edge of the pond again.

Now make a SONG OF THE FROGS.

Sing it together sitting on the edge of the pond. Make it a tuneless song.

Sing about your frog magic. What sounds and words could you use?

Make a LOT OF SOUND. Record the result.

a) Practise by making the same sound altogether, at the same time.
   e.g. CROAK, CROAK, CROAK.

b) Then practise making a variety of sounds or words simultaneously,
   so there are lots of sounds sounding all at once, as in the illustration
   above.

(Give a start and stop signal for this.)

LION

Visualization

Imagine the heat of a hot wide grasslands; grass as tall and soft as the fur of a lion.

Movement

1. Everyone in their own space.

Stand your ground

Lion is large and powerful,

Feel the strength of lion in YOU

Stand with legs apart

Knees bent and arms wide

And now altogether with one big sound...

R O A R

2. Everyone travelling.

Then move silently with big soft movements....

keep your body large....

as you:

PAD ALONG

ROLL and

LEAP

3. Then move in threes or fours FOLLOWING A LEADER.
   Move slowly, keep the sequences clear and simple. Decide on a signal for when the next person in line becomes the leader so you all have a turn at being the lion king.

4. Imagine night is coming. How will the group finish? Lions SLEEPING?

SNAKE

With a partner

1.   TWIST around each other

Find ways of curling and stretching

Over, under and around

UP and DOWN

Not touching but skilfully near

Moving your bodies as if you are

BONELESS but STRONG.

2.   Find some body sculptures as if you both together make

ONE SNAKE

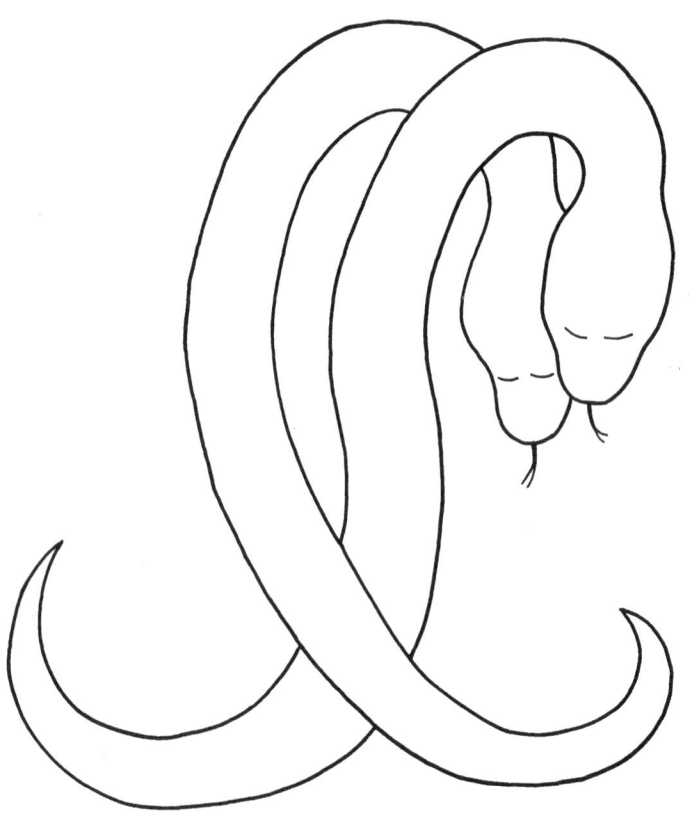

THE DANCE

The dance may begin after the choosing of the cards and when the animals are in their designated STARTING POSITIONS:

1. All the animals are in their chosen starting positions in the body shape of their animal.
Imagine that the animals have been called upon and they have come from the depths of the forest to bring their animal medicine.

(Faint background music can be played throughout).

2. The animals find their animal tribe – travelling into their four groups.

3. Each group of animals is designated a space and one group performs at a time, being guided by the percussive accompaniment of:

DEER   woodblock rhythms

FROG   the recorded 'song' which the frogs can join in with at
        the end of their dance.

LION   a deep toned drum or tambour

SNAKE   hissing sounds, recorded or live

Depending on the length of the sequences, (3) above might be repeated or overlapped and the spatial relationships between the groups clarified (for example the deer might be trotting round the frogs).

All the groups finish holding their animal shapes still.

Ending the dance
Finally now we will call on EAGLE.

EAGLE

The most powerful bird in the sky

Who is able to grant wishes

And manifest the magic.

Everyone slowly begins a unison SOFT STAMPING to the sound of a drumbeat and gradually moves into the centre of the space and forms into one big group to represent the body of Eagle.

Lean forward, open your arms wide like wings,

Stamp your feet

More, more. Listen to the drum
And now

SILENCE, STILLNESS

The animals have spoken. The dance is ended.

What was it like to become the animal?

What message or magic are you and the animals bringing to the world?
Tell each other about your message......

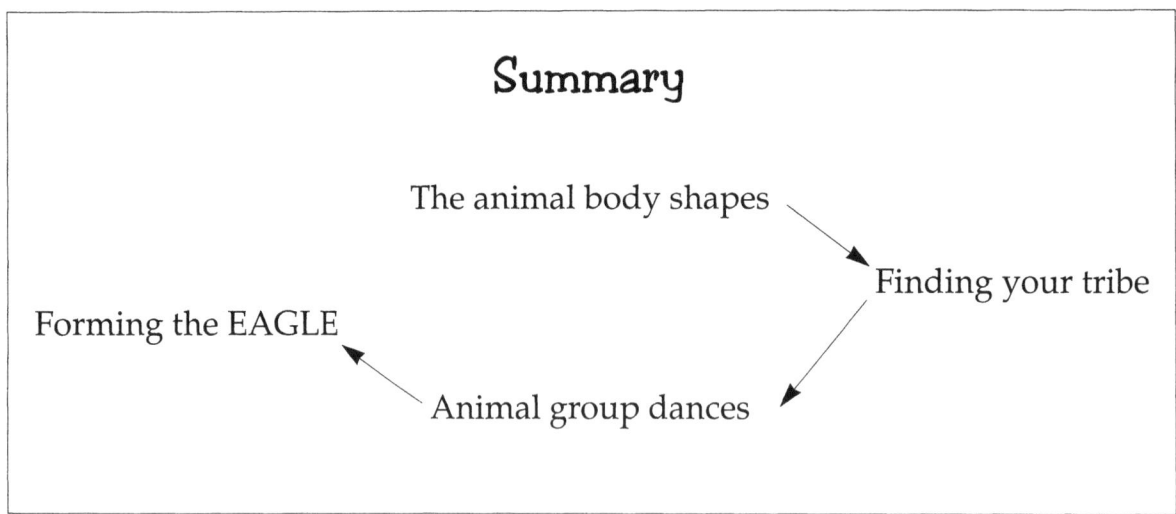

Costumes and designs

Paint or fabric print on old white T-shirts, a picture of your animal or alternatively of the animal's surroundings, e.g. forest or water.

For a performance, paint your face with FACE PAINTS.

Make yourself look amazing!

Read

Medicine Cards by Jamie Sams and David Carson (Bear & Company, New Mexico) for more information on North American beliefs.

Endnote

The underlying ideas in this chapter, which was stimulated by ancient North American Indian beliefs and rituals, have been used in work with both adults and children. This chapter is dedicated to Terry Cooper, who first introduced me to the *Medicine Cards*.

MYSELF

The underlying belief here is that we can learn about ourselves through movement and related arts and that deeper awareness of ourselves inevitably leads to deeper awareness of the world in which we live.

The emphasis is on both the individual and the group, on both dancing yourself and collaborating with others. The suggested art activities interweave with the movement, the one stimulating and enriching the other.

So we begin with:

1. Visualization and breathing

2. INDIVIDUAL movement, encouraging movement exploration and variety leading to:

3. ART activities – making Body Maps about 'Myself'
These are large, life size drawings that could be displayed near the dance like a backcloth around the walls of the movement space.

It is fun and invigorating to work LARGE, but if this is not practical, make smaller drawings or paintings of 'Myself' instead.

4. Consolidating individual movement sequences arising from the movement and the art ideas of (2) and (3)

5. Making GROUP dances in 4's.

1. Visualization

I am my body.

My body is myself.

I am also my

Thoughts, feelings, memories and

Imaginings.

I am my

Inside and my outside.

I am part of my

Family, community and

the whole

WORLD.

I am a

Cell

of the

Universe.

Encourage thoughts and responses to the idea of MYSELF
e.g. Who is myself?
What do I look like?
Where do I live?
What do I like?

Then focus very much on AWARENESS of MYSELF and my MOVEMENT.
Do this through the above visualization and the following breathing exercise.

Breathing

I breathe. If I close my eyes I can just focus on my breathing.

If I do that quietly for a few minutes I can begin to notice my whole body.

Now I can feel my feet, toes, legs, stomach, back, shoulders.........all the parts of my body. I can practise breathing into them, as if I breathe them into life.

Encourage a brief discussion after the visualization and breathing about how all the parts of the body can MOVE.
e.g. Arms stretching, back bending, feet jumping, shoulders shrugging etc.

2. Individual movement

Encourage everyone to move freely in their own very individual way, finding many CONTRASTING ways of moving.

A lively piece of music here could be used to accompany.
e.g. Exploring quick movements, or flowing 'river' movements.

Encourage continuous movement, spontaneity and variety and the repetition of interesting ideas.

Begin by reading out the following verse or while they are moving call out an idea as a further stimulus.

All the parts of my body can move.

Moving quickly

or

s l o w l y.

with LARGE movements

or small.

I can be ALIVE with movement

like a river,

like a bird,

like an animal,

or still as a cloud.

My feet are dancing, my arms, back and head,

dancing to the music

dancing to the feeling inside me

dancing MYSELF.

It is very important to observe and appreciate each person's ideas – perhaps half the class moving at a time with a spirit of cooperation and curiosity about the movement. Sometimes everyone could practise one person's idea.
Everyone now lies down and rests for a few minutes and remembers their movement and their ideas.

What did you notice or enjoy about your movement? What did you see, imagine or remember about yourself?
e.g. "That movement reminds me of………."
    Which movements went well together or felt new or exciting?
    How did you dance YOURSELF?

They will need to remember these ideas later (see page 30). Maybe they could make a list of the ideas now.

3. Art activities
Now we change the activity from moving to drawing and make body maps:

Body maps
The idea here is to draw round the OUTLINE of the body and then to colour it, decorate it etc.

You need:
a roll of lining paper,
sticky tape, scissors,
crayons, chalks or felt pens.
or paint, bits of fabric, coloured paper (crêpe paper is useful for making 'clothes'), glue

Cut two lengths of paper the height of the person to be drawn around and then tape the two pieces together side by side. (A roll of lining paper could be used.)

With a partner:
One of you lie down on the paper. Your partner draws round you very carefully, so that your outline is clear on the paper. You have to lie very still for this and try to draw close to the shape of the body.

Then change roles so that each of you has a life size drawing of yourself.

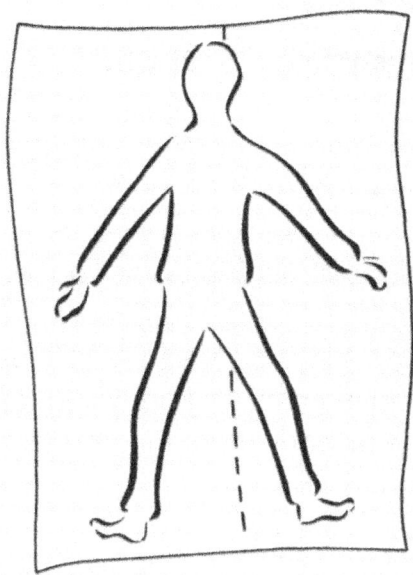

Now sit beside your paper for a few moments and remember all the movements and ideas you had as you moved and thought about yourself...............................then

Put the movement ideas onto your body map making perhaps colourful patterns to represent the movement.
e.g. 'I am all black and red twisting and turning.'
Decorate and colour in your outline in your own way. Select from a range of media e.g. paint, crayons, coloured paper, fabric.

You can change your body map and turn it into a particular image
e.g. a spaceman, or a fantastic bird,
or
'This is me roller skating or running or playing'
or

Anything you like, just so that you feel that it represents you and **your movement** in some way –

In addition you could write on your body map about yourself.
It's a BODY MAP of YOU.

If possible, before moving again, arrange these body maps as wall hangings in the movement space so that you can move near them. Or if you hang them in the classroom, take a good look at them before moving again, i.e. make connections between the visual work and the movement work.
(If you use stiff paper you could also cut round the body outline and suspend or arrange the cut out body shapes.)

4. Consolidating movement

(Putting together the movement and the art work)

Take a good look at your body map. Remember all those wonderful movement ideas you explored earlier (page 28).

You may think of a few more movement ideas as you look at your body map.

Now SELECT just a few ideas to make clear sequences of movement.
You need only a handful of movements and body shapes now to describe in movement who you are (on your body map and in movement).

e.g.

"I'm like a red and black snake twisting and turning."

"I like to leap, run and balance as I play."

"I am very energetic"

"This is my quiet side."

"I am a fantastic bird."

"I like computers."

Work out your own individual sequences for your idea.

Practise them and show them to each other.

THE DANCE

Now you are going to share your ideas with others in groups of four. Each of you takes a turn at leading the group with your own individual sequence.

Make Groups of Four
If possible, group yourselves in relationship to your body maps, not necessarily close to them.

You might, for example, begin in a line all looking towards your four maps.

Each of you choose a STARTING POSITION connected to your own idea.

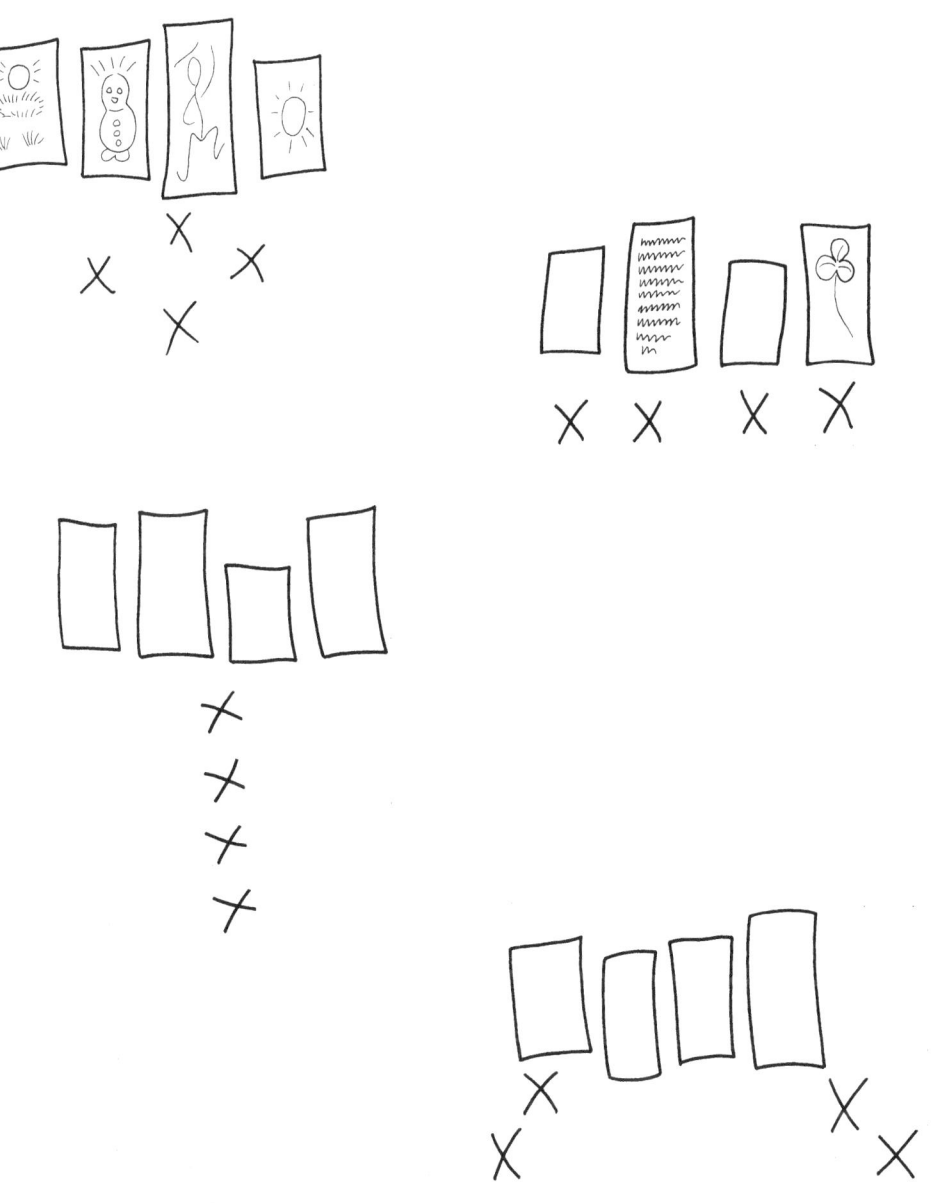

Then each in turn -
Take turns to LEAD the group movement through moving your own chosen sequence lots of times.

The others in your group can mirror you, doing the same action
e.g. all rising, turning and stretching out. Or the group can reflect the *quality* of your movement, e.g. moving very softly high and low, or moving energetically and strongly rather than copying the same action. Keep going so the rhythmic quality grows.

Suggest 'Moving like each other', so that the interpretation need not be too rigid.

It's like bringing the body maps ALIVE.

Each person takes a turn to lead so that there are FOUR SECTIONS of movement, each led by a different person, each very individual.
The beginnings and endings of the four movement sections should be clearly defined.

Each group might perform their dance alone or several might perform simultaneously.

Ending the dance
After the fourth sequence everyone holds their ending position very still and calls out their NAME and ADDRESS, loudly and simultaneously, three times as if you
are saying –

This is who

WE ARE !

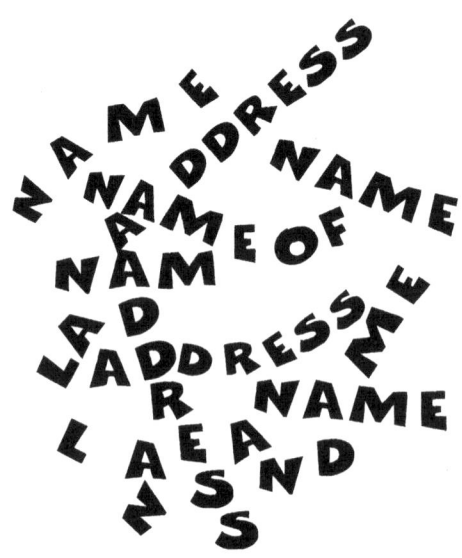 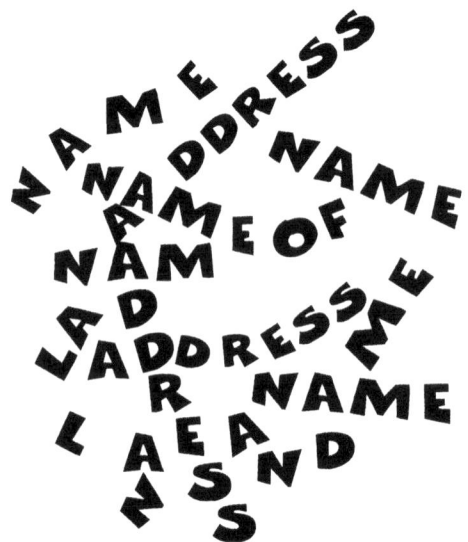

Try "Ready altogether, call out your name and address, NOW."
Use a hand gesture to start the sound off.

32

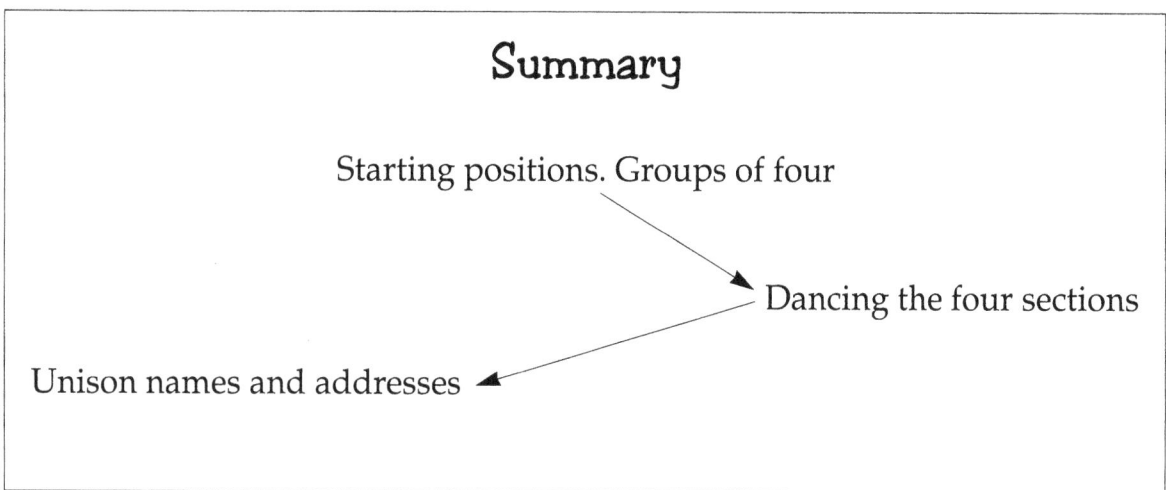

Summary

Starting positions. Groups of four

Dancing the four sections

Unison names and addresses

Related activities

Finding out about the anatomy and physiology of the body (how am I made up?)

Writing about memories, incidents, wishes or hopes for MYSELF or MY LIFE.

Endnote

The theme of 'Dancing Yourself' and the interrelationship between movement, art work and language has been central to my work.

A STORY IN MOVEMENT

Read or tell the story to the class.
Perhaps read it a second time with everyone with their eyes closed imagining themselves moving and then beginning to pick out the interesting movement ideas in each section of the story. Of course Tiel might equally well be a boy.

The Girl and the Turtle

Once there was a girl called Tiel who lived in a place where the sun was warm all the year round. Every day she would help her parents fish in the sheltered waters of the lagoon. One day she was walking slowly along **the seashore** scuffing her toes into the sand and occasionally splashing in and out of the water, when she saw ahead of her a great turtle on the shoreline, moving very gently in the water.

She stood very still. Then she heard a strange, low pitched sound. She knew suddenly that she could understand the sound just as if it were words only more mysterious. The turtle was asking her to climb on its back and dive with it deep **down to the sea bed**. In a moment she had agreed and gripping the shell tightly was taken down through the water, like falling, like floating, floating-falling, her hair streaming above her, bubbles sliding past her skin.

They stopped, so gently it was hardly noticeable. Fearlessly she floated off the turtle's back. He waited as she drifted away to explore this strange, watery landscape....She travelled along **exploring the sea bed**, sometimes rolled, sometimes lifted or outstretched by currents and eddies. She slid under rocks, crouched by huge waving sea plants and once, in slow motion, ran after a shoal of silver fishes.

Then before her there was a **cave** like an enormous circle of darkness before her, fringed with light green sea grass. There was the sound again, now a low booming which filled her ears and mind. It told her she was invited into the cave. There were mysteries there, unknown things and more than things, ideas, thoughts and feelings; wonderful ideas which you could choose from, anything you wanted. It was a Transformation Cave. She knew this. In the darkness she could not see but she could feel with her hands, the shapes and sizes and beautiful textures, like silk or smooth stone or soft sea foam and whisper to herself all the ideas that she could hear now inside her head.

She chose one thing to take with her from the cave, something very important to her, very special just for her. And then,
> twisting and turning and floating
> reaching out with her arms and
> kicking with her legs
she travelled back to the turtle and then **returned** up, up to the surface of the water again, splashing into the shallows and lying on the beach, in her mind's eye seeing and feeling once more the wonders of below the sea.

She kept for always what she brought from the cave. It made her happy. If ever she felt depressed or alone she could in her imagination go down with the turtle to that special place beneath the waves.

Making movement

Focus on the movement creativity using the story to provide atmosphere and encourage different movement qualities. Give plenty of time to each section.

On the seashore

1. Imagine now you are WALKING on soft sand.......walking

   slowly......placing your heel down, ball of the foot, then the toes,

   pausing sometimes.......and perhaps sometimes stretching up towards

   the sun or curling down to touch the sand gently with

   your hands.......making a sequence of movements of your own.

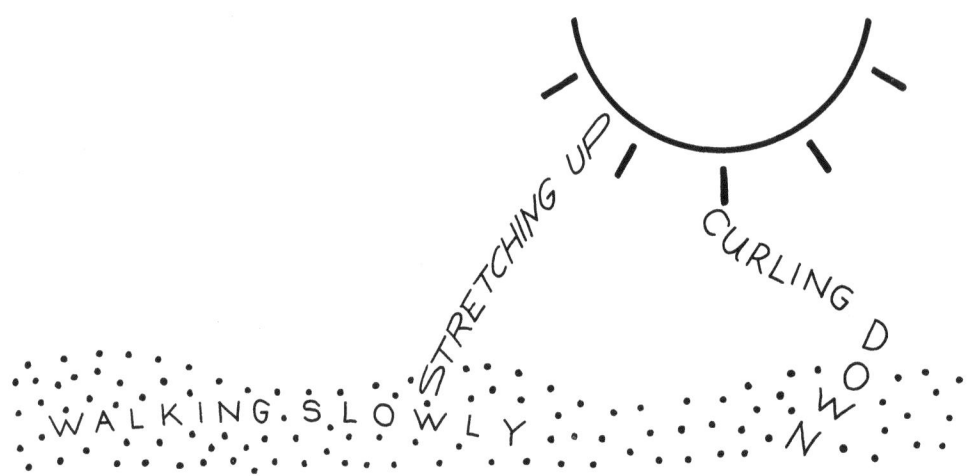

2. You could interrupt this every so often by a quick, rushing, movement into the sea and add a high leap or 'splash' arm gesture. Maybe in this part you would all be in unison, all on the same rhythm so this phrase is a dynamic contrast to the walking.

   For example: Walking slowly for six steps, then

   Turn, Run and JUMP with

   Knees and hands high......

   As you land, bring the palms of your hands

   down sharply as if SPLASHING the surface

   of the water.

Down to the sea bed

F
   A
     L
       L
         I
           N
             G

In stillness, imagine sinking down through the water with the turtle.

Imagine falling movements before you fall.

Then prepare to fall.....wait....then fall slowly, diving or crumpling, knowing when each part of your body moves, falls, slowly, part by part.

Imagine there is endless falling.So that you rise up to fall again, finding a phrase, feeling into what you are doing, fitting in with others around you, not the exact same movement but everyone slow and falling.

Then pausing, hardly moving...

Stillness.

Exploring the sea bed

Now is an opportunity to make a follow my leader dance. Follow your partner. Explore the sea bed together.

Go up, go down – make your journey very clear, your body shape clear, your direction clear, using:

Soft rolling,

sliding, under and over

reaching out,   crouching,   slow motion running

Wait for your partner, so that you move like in mirrors.
Sometimes one leads, sometimes the other – change leader without a word spoken – become like one person.

Finish very still, like two underwater statues.

In the cave

Now is the time when you all find something precious to you, perhaps something you have always wanted.

It does not have to be an object. It might be a feeling or a wish or an event. Let your imagination have its way.

Through movement *anything* is possible.

You could wish to be King or Queen or fly anywhere, real or imaginary.

First you must SEARCH with your hands through the dark of the cave, gently moving your hands up, down, around, until you find what is precious to you. This part of your movement could be quite short, a phrase repeated a couple of times and then, hold still....

Now how can you indicate with your position, your body shape, what it is that you have found?

You might be holding something in your hands or showing a particular mood or.....what ideas are there here?

Everyone will be different. Take some time to see each one.

The return

Now with the turtle once more,

float,

reach upwards

and return to lie on the beach again.

Rest there.

Remember all that you have done and what you have found.

Making accompaniment – turtle sounds

The sound of the turtle, "a strange, low pitched sound."

1. Try singing these sounds, very low pitched and slow -

OOOOO AAAAA EEEEE OOOOO.....
EEEEE OOOOO AAAAA EEEEE.....

OOO – as in 'pool'
AAA – as in 'park'
EEE – as in 'eat'.

Keep repeating them so the room reverberates with this low, slow sound.

2. Then divide into three groups. Each group starts on a different sound as in a 'round' so that there are different vowels sounding simultaneously, as in the above diagram.

You can play around with this idea for ages....different length sounds, different pitches.

3. *Also* try............. whispering the sounds to make whispery music.

For the suggested dance you will need
a length of low pitched sounds (as in 1. and 2.)
and also
a length of whispered sounds (as in 3.)

Tape record a length of this voice music and use it to accompany sections of movement as suggested in The Dance, page 42.

Or have half the group making the sounds and half the group moving.

Later when you bring ideas together, the whole dance could open with this sound – a mysterious beginning.

Preparing to put it all together

Remember – these are the parts you have practised:

On the seashore

Falling

Exploring

The Cave

The Return

    and

Turtle Sound

All these sections have different movements and moods. You can practise any of them in any order.

Perhaps practise different parts simultaneously, as individuals or in groups, refining the ideas, clarifying rhythms, discovering new possibilities, taking plenty of time to deepen the work.

It's rather like editing a film, sorting out how to put the dance together.

Here is a possible format.

In your mind's eye imagine ....The Dance

THE DANCE

On the seashore

The dance begins in stillness, everyone motionless in a position from the **On the seashore movement**.

The sound of turtle can be heard faintly. Then the motionless figures on the sand come alive, everyone moving fully.
(Play the low turtle sound very quietly.)
As the turtle sound gradually increases (*crescendo*), people slowly stop their movement and listen, keeping very still until the sound is really loud.

Falling

One by one or group by group, begin **falling**, down to the sea bed..........

Exploring

You turn towards towards your partner and begin **exploring the sea bed**.

In the cave

(Play the whispery section here.)
The sound of turtle stops you once again. This time the sound is different, all whispery and mysterious. You all turn towards the centre of the space as if this is the dark **cave** and in your imagination step into it..... Now to find the precious thing – hands moving up and down – *not much travelling here* – until each person holds in stillness the precious something that they have found.

Ask them to hold the body shape connected to their idea. eg They might literally be holding something in their hands. They may have momentarily transformed into a ......magic fish. Ask them "What have you found? Show me with your body."

The return

With one unison movement you **rise back up** to the surface of the water again. You pause there, then form a circle.

There you imagine you are gently holding your precious thing, or idea, in the palm of your hands and lift it high in the air. Then one after the other, around the circle you repeat the lifting high movement and say out loud what it is you have brought from the sea bed, and the others in the circle repeat this quietly after you.

The dance could end here or you could add the following circle dance.

To end, celebrate all these wonderful things with a circle dance; skipping or stamping faster and faster to a quickening drumbeat. And behind it all the sound of the turtle growing louder and then gradually dying away into silence so the dance finishes with the sound of the turtle.

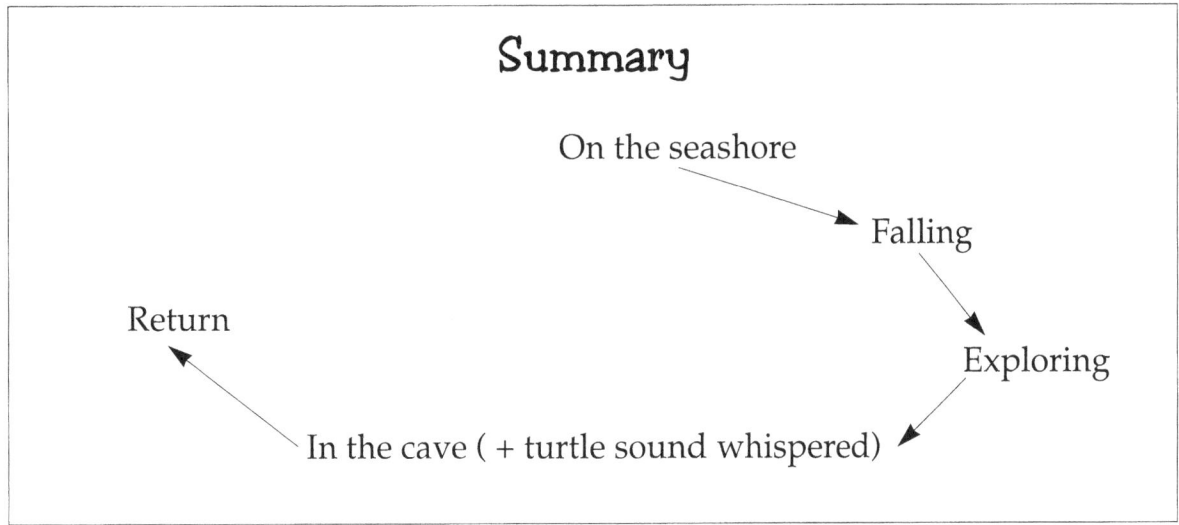

Summary

On the seashore

Falling

Exploring

In the cave (+ turtle sound whispered)

Return

Turtle sound accompaniment

You will need to make three sections of sound as on page 40 and use them at will. Use crescendo *and* diminuendo *to give variety to the sound.*

Endnote

The imaginary landscape in this chapter arises from diverse memories of moving by the sea e.g. A Beach Dance Project on the Dwynnan Peninsula, North Wales for a mixed group, including those with special needs.

WHEELS

This chapter is a challenge to imagination, inventiveness and skill. The emphasis is on the development of movement sequences which arise as the wheel image powers free flowing movement. Wheels are not interpreted literally but suggest movement using the shape, flowing quality and associations of the wheel. The feeling of the movement and how the idea of 'wheel' can stimulate one movement leading to another, and one group formation to another, is the nub of the idea. In encouraging the ideas, link images to movement words and play with the variety of movement response to them.

For example: A wheel gathering speed might suggest a slow deep circling turn, leading into a floor roll gathering speed, into a quick jump to the feet and three whirling arm movements.
'Wheels' is an example of in-depth exploration from one initial image.

There are many symbolic meanings of wheel and wheel as circle. In the Eastern world the wheel is a symbol of spirituality and for many people it has a deep rooted significance apart from the obvious. In today's car culture, the wheel is often a symbol of power and freedom.

Brainstorm the ideas:

Imagine all the wheels there are. Wheels everywhere on..

CARS

BUSES

MOTORBIKES

BICYCLES

WINDMILLS

MACHINERY

WHAT ABOUT HOOPS?

WHEELS   TURNING   SPINNING   MOVING

What would we do without them?

44

Visualization

Close your eyes for a moment...

Imagine wheels

The shape of the wheel

The MOVEMENT of the wheel.

Wheels moving slowly

Gathering speed or

Skidding to a halt

What do you imagine if you think of wheels?

Write down the suggestions on a large piece of paper. You can use them later in the Game in section 3 (page 48 where you call out an image that 'wheels' suggest and the children must quickly respond in movement).

Making movement

1. By yourself

All the joints of your body can in turn be the centre of a wheel circling movement. Make yourself into a HUMAN WHEEL!

Circle your arm from the shoulder

Reaching out into the space

Lead circles with your elbow

One side and the other

Circle your head

Reach high with your fingertips

And make a big wheel movement with your whole body

Up, forward, down and behind

Make circles all around your body

Try using noses, knees

Rolling and cartwheels

Get wheeling!

Mix and match these ideas together. Make a skilful INDIVIDUAL sequence led by different parts of your body. Be adventurous.

Give everyone a chance to show their wheel inventions.

2. With a partner

Making wheel movements together.

Explore ways of moving together where you hold hands and **support each other's weight**. Do this slow motion to begin with and very carefully.
E.g.
Hold hands and lean away from each other a little
Spin together slowly at first and then more quickly.

or

One person, A, is like the hub of the wheel and stays on the spot.
The other one, B, holds their hand. Both lean away – arms outstretched.
B moves around their partner – running and dipping up and down, like the roundabout at a funfair.

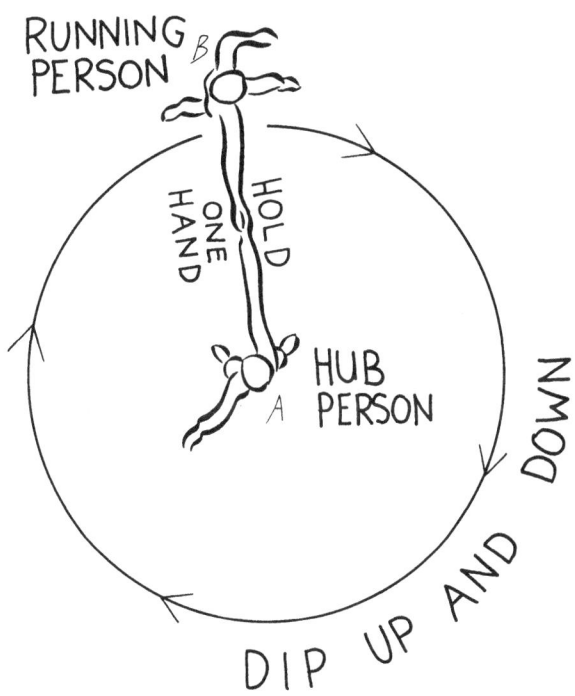

Experiment with other ways of making HUMAN WHEELS with your partner.

More suggestions

Stretching circles, reaching high and low.

Rolling or spinning together

Moving around each other
side by side or back to back.

Imagine racing wheels

Or moving slow and large

Like a windmill

In a breeze.

Choose a few contrasting phrases of movement to do together.

3. Make GROUPS OF SIX

Comprised of THREE of the above PAIRS from the previous section (2, with a partner) and spread well out in the space.

Now for a B I G   W H E E L IMAGE made out of your whole group; LIKE a GROUP WHEEL.

a) First of all we will practise this idea as a GAME. You have to think what sort of group shape comes to mind: huge, long, low or high etc.

The teacher calls out an image e.g.

A WATER WHEEL or BUS

or RACING CAR or AEROPLANE

or PENNY FARTHING or TANK

or WINDMILL

Each group must quickly respond and form themselves into a GROUP SHAPE to interpret the image. Refer to the suggestions that emerged after the visualization (page 45). Call out the idea e.g. "aeroplane."

Without discussion the group (of 6) quickly moves into their idea of the Aeroplane shape. It is a test of ingenuity and speed and fun to do. It does not have to be too literal! You will need this group shape later to begin the dance.

*Then each group chooses which group shape idea they like best. That is **their** chosen group shape.*

b) Now beginning in your chosen group shape, begin to find some movements which you do altogether in unison. This is your GROUP WHEELS MOVEMENT.

Make some phrases of movements. Finish again with a very clear group shape, one that you could remember and return to.

For example, from the Windmill shape, phrases of movement could evolve such as:
(i) All the group circling both arms in the same direction
(ii) Beginning one after the other, circling one arm then the other arm, varying the level and direction of the movement – some circling high, some low – all fitting in together, so the group is a mass of circling arms.
(iii) Evolving a movement holding hands.

Add some voice sound to the movements.
Show your idea one group at a time.

4. Hoops
Finally now choose one of the groups of six people to bowl hoops.

One at a time, from different directions, practise bowling a hoop smoothly across the space. Try this at different speeds. How skilful can you be?

THE DANCE

Each group of six (three couples) has its own dance, beginning in its chosen group shape. Within the group each person moves first individually, then with their partner, then with the whole group. The scene is set by beginning the dance with six people bowling the HOOPS across the space to symbolise the theme of wheels.

1. To set the scene, six people bowl the hoops across the space.

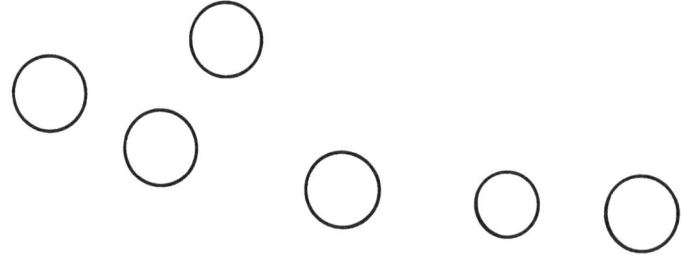

Hoops

2. While in your GROUP shapes, hold your positions very still (as page 49).

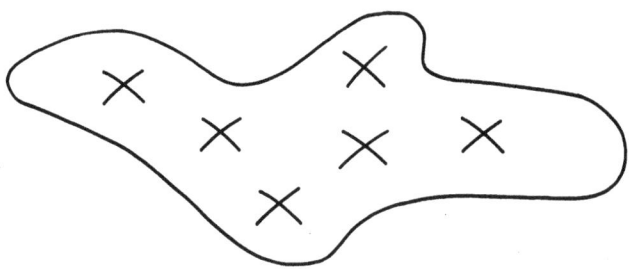

Group shape

3. Now in your group move **near** each other but moving your own INDIVIDUAL, favourite wheel sequences practised earlier.
   You can all be different.
   At a signal, interrupt your movement and hold it still.

Moving individually

Turn to your partner and...

Then perform:

4. PARTNER wheels. Move your partner creations.

Partner work   X X   X X   X X

Pause. Turn back to your group and form your group shape once more...
Then perform:

5. The GROUP wheels sequence. Begin and end this in your group shape.

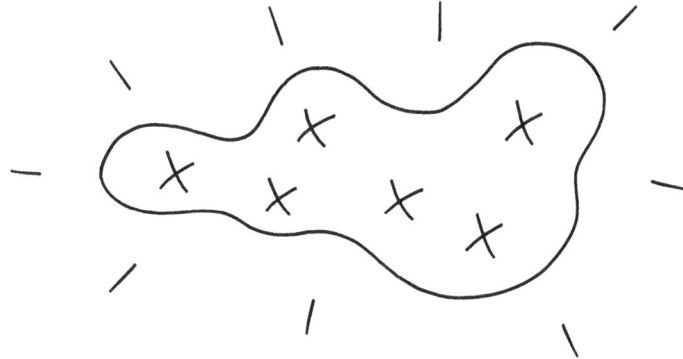

Moving as a group (e.g. racing car, aeroplane)

So the dance order is

HOOPS BOWLING and GROUP SHAPES *Everyone still except for those bowling hoops*

INDIVIDUAL SEQUENCES *Move gently away into individual sequences*

PARTNER WORK *Find your partner, move together*

GROUP WHEELS MOVEMENT *Go back into your group shape and then your group movement*

Perhaps to END there is one hoop bowled amongst the groups and then....

CRASH

all the wheels

COLLAPSE!

Summary

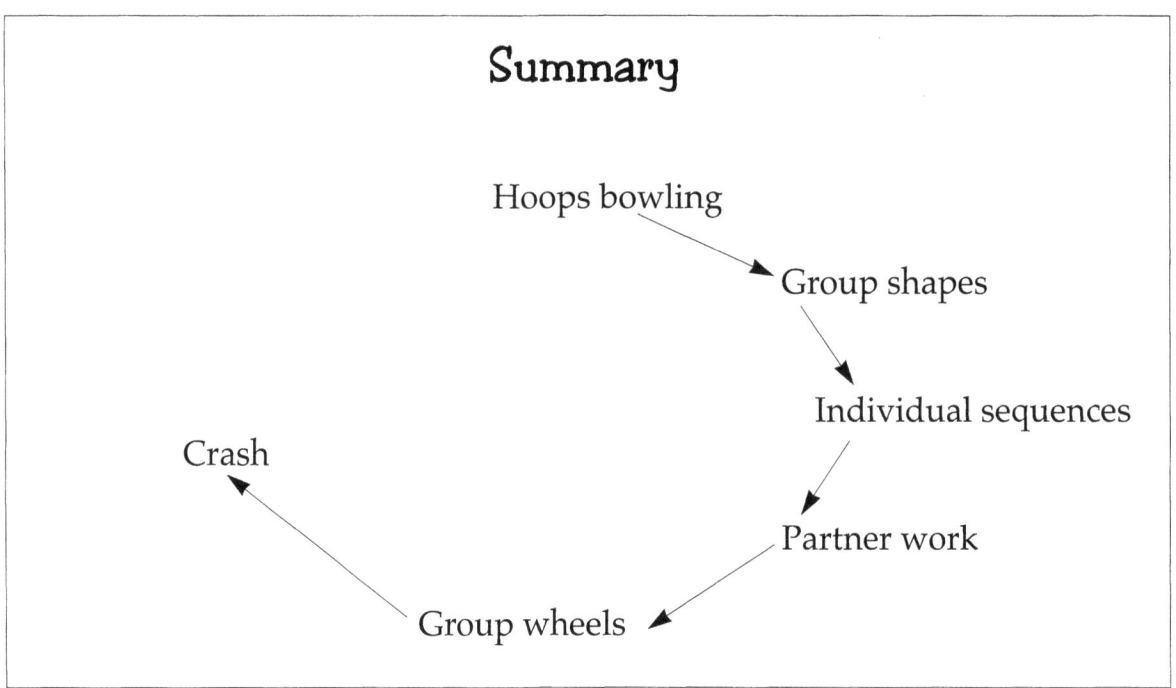

Hoops bowling

Group shapes

Individual sequences

Crash

Partner work

Group wheels

Accompaniment

Make a tape. Tape record a collage of voice sounds or traffic sounds. Intersperse these with information about the history of wheels or opinions about wheels today.

Use the above accompaniment like a backcloth to the movement.
Use a percussion instrument to guide the start of each section.

It is also quite simple to make a continuous 'whirling' sound by whirling a piece of thin plasic tubing overhead plus gentle thrumming on a cymbal, plus spinning the 'wheels' on a tambourine. Experiment.

Link to a project on Wheels – practical, symbolic, history of.

Collect photographs, drawings, actual wheels, wheel hubs.

Construct a giant collage or wheel sculpture. Install this as part of the performance.

Endnote
Dedicated to Bosco Oliveria, percussionist, with vivid memories of whirling circles. In performances and workshops for children and young people throughout the UK.

DREAMS

Our dreams come from deep inside us. As we sleep they drift into our minds like a picture underworld. Our dreams may have a variety of meanings for us. In many cultures, dreams are considered very important. For Australian Aboriginals for example, dreams are guides and inspiration for everyday living. Dreams contain symbols which, like signposts, show us more clearly what we only half know.

The dream can be a source of movement. You could all **invent** a dream together. Reflecting on and sharing dreams can be an introduction to the movement work.

We are all alone when we dream, alone in the world inside our heads, but when we move we can invite other people to share our dream. We can change it if we want to.

This chapter offers a variety of ideas for selecting movement ideas from dreams. A particular dream has been chosen, but of course many other dream scenarios are possible.

In the **Making movement** section, the idea of an individual dream circle is used to designate a personal space for movement exploration.

The *Making movement* part is aimed at encouraging lots of response to the different parts of the dream from which an individual choice of movements is then made.

On the following page is a dream description. It might be one person's dream or a composite of dreams from different people.

Read it out loud.

The Dream

Listen to the dream....

We are climbing a brown spiral staircase. We climb and climb, twisting and turning upwards, climbing to the very top.

Then at last when we do arrive there is nothing ahead... only endless space. We feel scared of falling...

Suddenly we take off into the air and fly. We're wheeling and flying, turning and airborne, high in the sky, looking down at the land far beneath us. This is fun!

Now so high up we get drawn into the sun – we actually become the sun, all joining together to make a huge, yellow, warm-centred sun with beaming rays of light radiating from it.

The sun explodes. We are fragments of sharp light shooting up, down, all sharp angles and energy.

Then we feel dragged down towards the earth. We are in a thick impenetrable jungle.

We struggle and twist and turn, caught up by a dark web of teeming plant life.

Slowly the jungle dissolves, flattens out and becomes a huge, warm, still pool in which we can float, resting, almost motionless.

What do you feel in this dream? What does it remind you of?

Making movement

To begin with you are going to mark out your movement space with a circle.

Begin to walk slowly in a circle, in a very dream like way.

In your own space, slowly walk in a circle, marking out your space. .

This is your **dream circle** that you are going to move in.

Stand in your circle and be ready to move the dream.

Use the following script, selected from the Dream story, to stimulate the movement ideas. Use the words to accompany the movement too i.e. repeat them as the children are moving.

Repeat each idea several times to encourage full, rhythmic involvement.

1. Climbing a brown spiral staircase

Begin walking now, in and around your circle, as if CLIMBING up steep stairs.

Make your own pathway, spiralling within the circle. Your arms could stretch and spiral in the space around you as you go.

Sometimes pause so everyone is pausing at different moments in their dream circle. Until you reach the top and

STOP

You BALANCE, balance up high,

Arms outstretched, leaning forward a little.

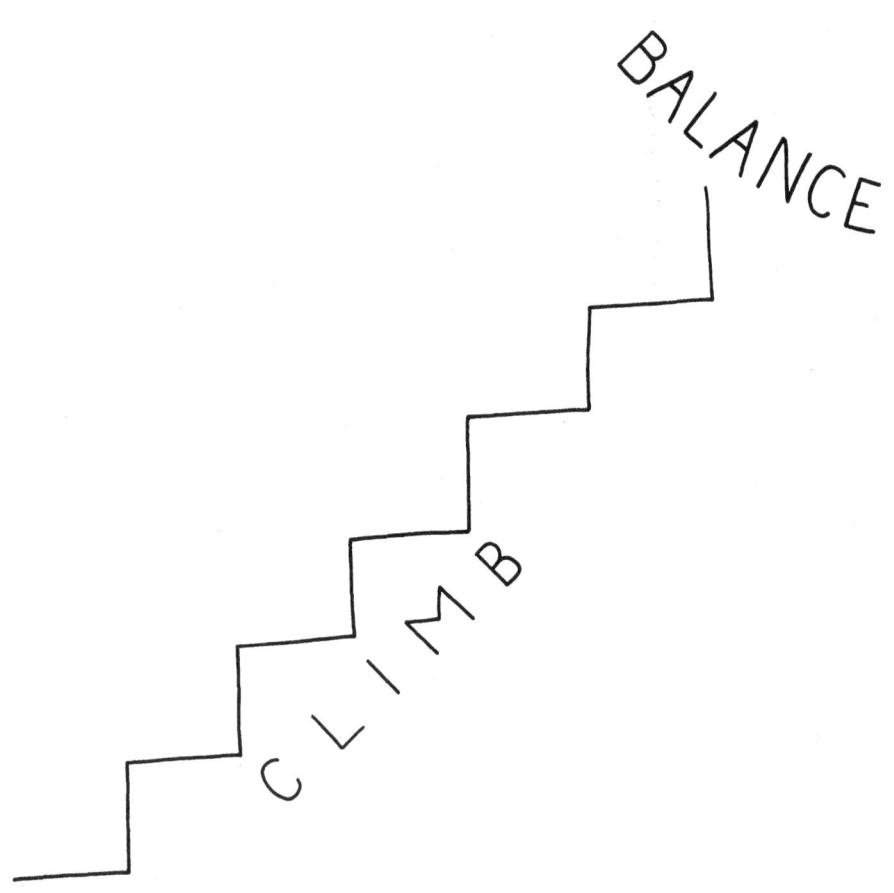

1. Climbing a brown spiral staircase

2. Into flying

Open your arms wide

LEAP, SWOOP and TURN

Fly in and out of the circle.

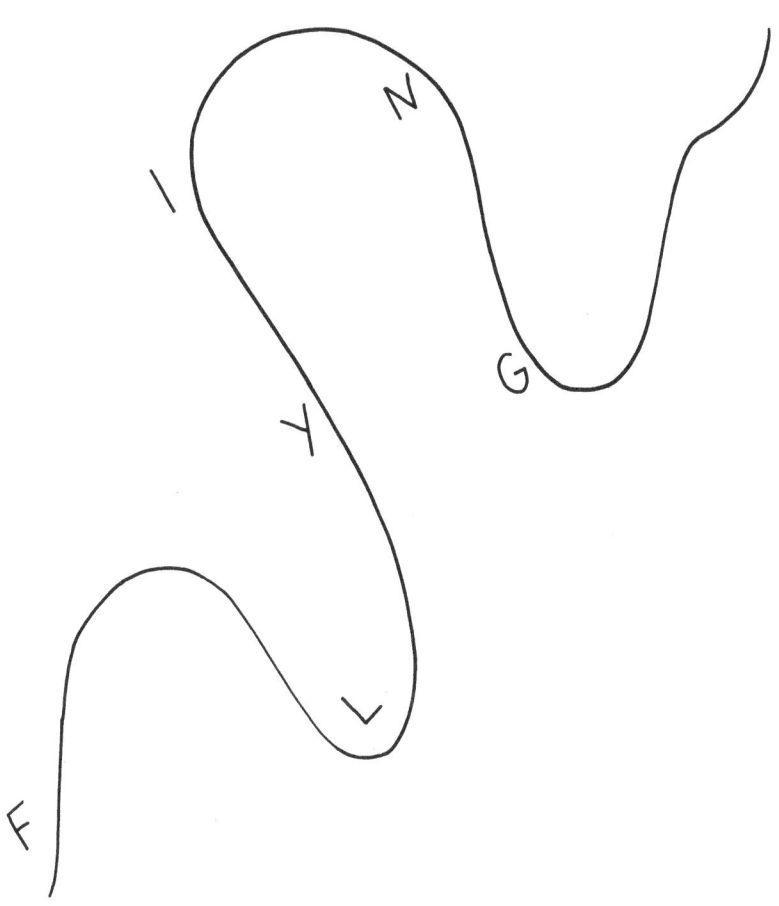

Keep wide, find flying steps and gestures

and then pause in your circle as the dream changes to....

...

3. The sun

All make the shape of the sun together;

From wherever you are find a way of

REACHING, stretching, towards the CENTRE of the space, like everyone is

radiating from the warm centre of the sun.

You can keep changing your stretch, leading the movement with different

parts of your bodies, like moving the heat of the sun.

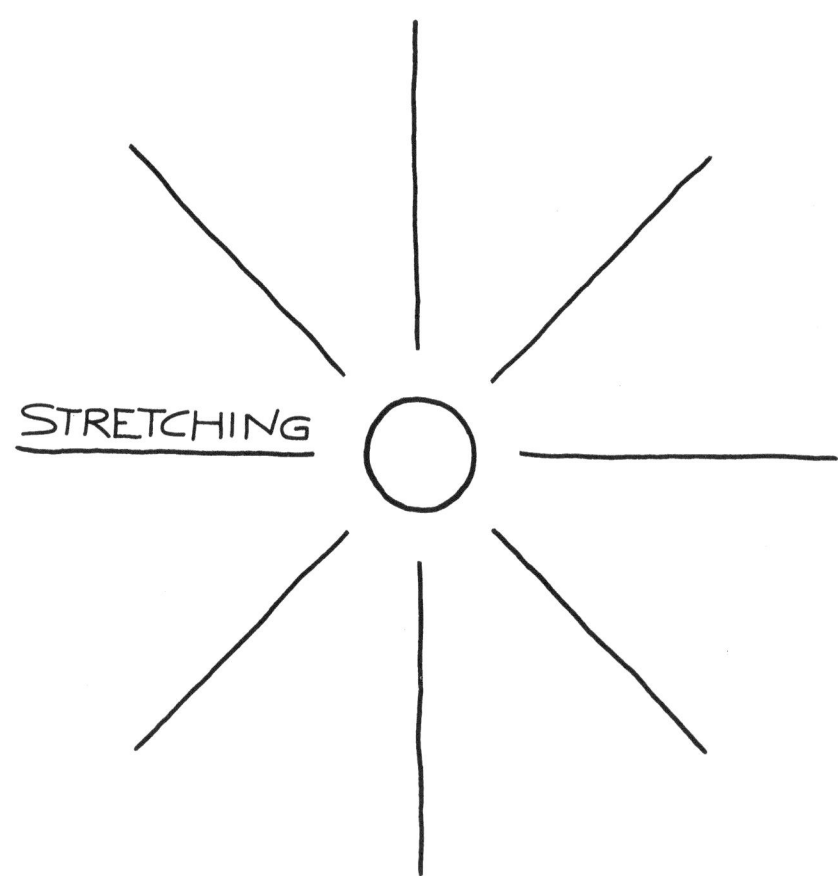

3. The sun

4. The sun explodes

SHOOT upwards suddenly; one, two or three sharp stretches or high

movements, finishing in a low broad position

before you are dragged down into.....

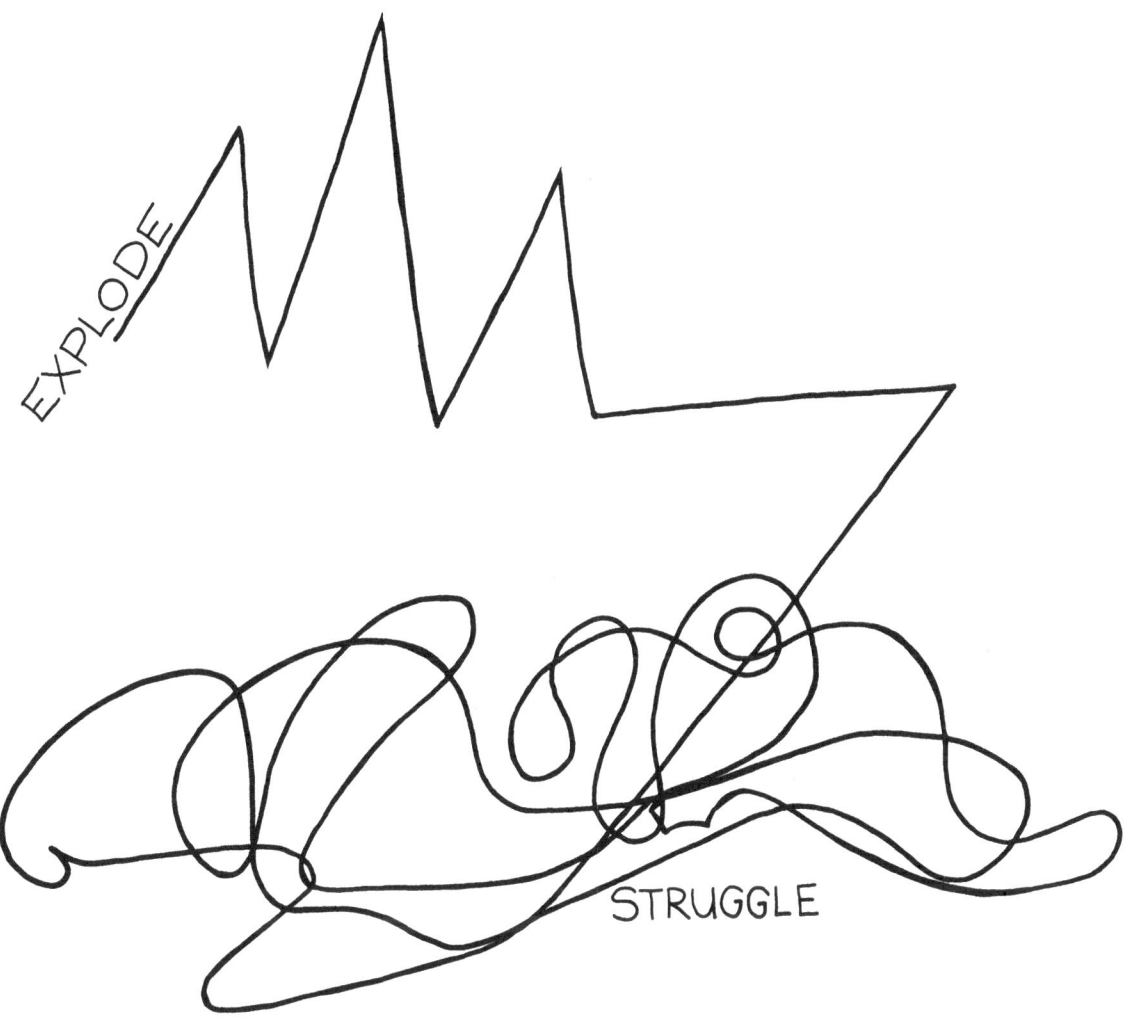

5. The jungle

Struggle, twist and turn.

Use your STRENGTH.

Use all the parts of your body.

Move up and down

Struggling and caught

By the jungle plants.

Now let all your energy MELT away as the restricting jungle dissolves...

6. Float......

........in the dream pool.

Let yourself gradually completely relax,

Floating on the surface of warm water.

F L O A T

For which part of the dream do you have the best movement ideas?

Developing the ideas

1. Select and repeat a phrase that you do ON YOUR OWN – individual movement.

Give everyone an opportunity to practise and develop a few phrases of movement from a PART of the dream, e.g. struggling, flying, or shooting upwards followed by floating – any combinations that feel good to do.

Then

2. THE WHOLE CLASS TOGETHER. Select ONE of these individual phrases. Decide together which one you would like to try out, one that everyone can roughly copy and perform altogether with UNISON movements and rhythm.

E.g. Everyone struggling and twisting with big twisting arm gestures, high and low. PAUSING .....
      ...... and then slowly, slowly, body part by body part sinking down to the ground to lie still in any 'floating' position.

In all, select two or three of these phrases to use later in The Dance.

4. BACKWARDS/DREAM - An additional idea

Let's make our dream go backwards! Backwards? Yes, backwards!

Do this by choosing body shapes from each part of the dream, and then snapping into them, one shape after another, only backwards to the original dream. So tell the dream story BACKWARDS ,

i.e. move into the shape of:

FLOATING (then freeze the shape)

STRUGGLING (then freeze the shape)

SHOOTING (then freeze the shape)

REACHING (then freeze the shape)

FLYING (then freeze the shape)

Play around with telling the dream backwards using body shapes. What is this experience like?

Encourage plenty of feedback and ideas here.
For other weird effects, try half the group moving the dream backwards, half forwards simultaneously!

DREAM DANCE

*Using these simple devices we can make the dream as straightforward or as strange as we like, **either***

by simply moving it straight through, as in the original dream story,
or
as below by fragmenting and changing the sequence of events in the dream so that it becomes more inconsequential and dreamlike to both experience and watch.

1. Everyone LIES DOWN quite still in their dream circle as if asleep.

2. Gradually everyone stands and begins to move their own favourite phrase from the dream, which they have practised earlier, so everyone is moving very INDIVIDUALLY at this point and many different parts of the dream are shown simultaneously.
It's like a DREAM COLLAGE, (see page 61).

Make this section short. Say "Begin now......Stop now"

3. Suddenly at a signal everyone is in UNISON (using the unison movements practised earlier) copying one person's phrase, as if the dream 'gets stuck', or like a dream 'follow my leader'.

Keep repeating the phrase. The movement could travel you about the room or stay 'on the spot'.

Then copy another, contrasting phrase. Practise several of these unison phrases.

4. Some backwards or forwards SHAPES – running the dream backwards and forwards, with quick, quick, quick changes of body shape (as page 62).

It does not matter whether the movement is logical – it probably is not! It is the dreamlike quick change that is important.
E.g.: • Snap from a floating shape to a struggling shape

   • A flying shape to a climbing-the-stairs shape....................*into:*

5. ....an....

........unexpected ending
Who knows what, because this is a dream and we can change our dreams.

Accompaniment

Find some ongoing, quiet background music for the Dream Dance and accent it with percussion to highlight the rhythm of the chosen movements.

Summary

1. Lying down asleep

2. A favourite phrase – every one different – individual movement

3. Unison phrases – every one the same

4. Backward / forward shapes

5. Unexpected ending.

Self decoration

Imagine yourself in the dream

What do you look like?

Use face paints

To transform yourself into

A SUN IMAGE or a

JUNGLE IMAGE

Make yourself
wierd and wonderful.

A relaxation
for the end of a lesson

Standing tall

Let your head drop forwards

Your shoulders, arms

Hang down towards the floor.

Bend your knees a little

Imagine a

WATERFALL

Is running down your back.

Then sink slowly

Down
To the floor.

Roll over onto

your back

And

Rest.

Endnote
An original version of Dreams was created as part of a combined arts project for a Special
school and a Primary school in Eastleigh, Hants

FEELINGS - A DANCE OF ANGER

Movement and feelings go together. Movement will often lead to a deeper connection to feelings and feelings will have a bodily or movement component. Often we can literally see how someone is feeling. In becoming more conscious of the connection between movement and feelings we can use the movement as a source of vivid ideas for dance making. Throughout, words are used as accompaniment. Encourage each child or group to have a simple, repeatable, clear phrase. Once these are established, lots of practice can happen in silence – saying the words inside you as you move.

Talking about feelings

Do you ever feel sad, happy, angry or afraid?

Your feelings are a part of you just as much as your arms and knees.

It can feel good to tell someone about how you feel.

Often you will find that they feel the same.

We're going to tell about our feelings through movement.

Let's take ANGER.

It's not OK to vent our anger on someone else or to hurt them,

but in movement we can express our anger and

use our anger energy safely and constructively

to produce a vivid and exciting dance.

Some introductory work using visualization and sound

First encourage body awareness, then, picturing/visualising anger-making things. Take plenty of time for this. Maybe ask them about their thoughts. Then encourage making the word phrases.

Sit with a straight back.

Feel the ground underneath you.

Feel strong as a rock.

Picture some things that

Make you angry ....

See them, feel them

And then

Slowly and softly

Begin to formulate some

Angry phrases:

I don't like that / leave me alone /

I won't eat that. etc. etc. etc.

Muttering at first
Then louder and LOUDER..until ..STOP

So speaking altogether you produce an amazing, powerful sound, all those different phrases sounding simultaneously.

Try that idea several times over.

Then still sitting,
begin to feel some movements in your body
that go with your words.

Move in a very small way as you sit.

Making movement

1. Alone

Make sure you have plenty of space around you. You can move as vigorously as you like in your own space but do not move into anyone else's space or touch anyone.

a) Choose one of your phrases. As you say the words begin to grow into a strong, angry body shape, as if you make yourself into an angry looking sculpture. e.g. with a wide stance, arms raised, fists clenched as you say loudly "I don't like that."

Repeat the phrase many times.

Find other contrasting angry body shapes high and low. Practise these, sometimes with the words, sometimes in silence.

b) Begin to fill out the movements leading into the shapes.
e.g. "Leave me alone".....A turn into a pushing shape
        "NO"........A leap into a strong, wide position

2. In pairs

a) Move alternately with your movement phrases and shapes – You move..I move... This is my phrase...Now your phrase. Give each other space. Let each of your ideas flow smoothly after the others.

b) Then choose a phrase of words that you can move TOGETHER at the same time, one you both agree with, not necessarily the identical movements, but fitting in with each other, feeling strong, looking POWERFUL e.g. "We are NOT going to bed."

Do this until you have made a chunk of movements and words with your partner, sometimes moving one after the other, sometimes simultaneously.

Everyone to take about the same amount of time for this (e.g. against a background of 30 slow taps on a drum). Encourage, knowing how you begin, make the body sculptures clear, clarify how it ends.

The idea content or motivation for the angry dances has deliberately not been specified. You may want to choose a particular topic and the words that arise from it (e.g. anger about pollution) or the dances may be very individual and personal.

3. Making a GROUP ANGER SCULPTURE

With your partner join two other couples, so now you are six. Then spread well out.

GROUPS OF SIX (3 pairs). Number yourself in the group – 1 to 6. You are going to move one after the other:

Number 1 moves into a strong shape

Number 2 joins 1 with either a reflecting or contrasting shape

Number 3 joins the first two likewise

Number 4 joins, then 5, then 6 until a strong group sculpture has been built up.

Demonstrate this idea with a group of six children, telling them when to move, with your voice or a tap on the drum:

> *First one.   ready....move and STILL*
> *Number two   ready....move and STILL*
>   *etc*

The essence is to move, join the group and hold still, one at a time.
Once the idea has been understood, you can practise and vary it over and over by the group forming and reforming. Add some angry words to the movement, (or you could of course start with the words as you did earlier).

Later on it is fun to forget about the numbering then and follow on spontaneously, quickly adapting to each other. Sometimes your group shape may remind you of something.

Look around. See the variety of sculptures and expressions there are in the space like group photographs of angry people.

4. The RHYTHM OF ANGER

Now we choose ONE phrase from any of those wonderful chants that you created – one that is meaningful to all of us – and we all begin to chant it together in unison – Then move as you chant it –

We say it with our voices

We say it with our feet...

Stamping and hopping.

Now with our arms

Swinging and clapping

Dancing the rhythm of

ANGER

Making ourselves be

Heard.

THE DANCE

Tape record a patch of muttered angry phrases as an introduction to the dance.

Preparation

Arrange all the participants standing with their partners in the space. Have everyone facing the BACK (upstage) so their faces cannot be seen.

facing upstage

1. EVERYONE BEGINS MUTTERING, adding their voices to the taped sound.

2. PARTNER DANCES. Gradually one couple turns to face front and begins moving their remembered angry phrases.

   Then quickly another couple, then another etc. so it's like a ripple of anger spreading through a crowd, perhaps like a lot of arguments about a lot of different things.

   Here all the partners will be moving simultaneously but with 'held' moments in their movement as they pause in their angry shapes.

Dancing with a partner

(Pause or fade the tape for stillness). Then 'cue in' the following section with a few taps on a drum.

3. GROUPS OF SIX. The group SCULPTURES practised earlier begin to form using their words and movement. (Make sure the three pairs are adjacent to each other at the beginning of the dance.)

These groups may perhaps be like 'pressure groups', all angry about a particular issue, for example:

"WE DON'T WANT ANY MORE MOTORWAYS"
    1   2   3   4   5   6

Decide how many times to repeat the group phrase (i.e. the building of the group structure), so that this section is very clearcut.

Group sculpture

4. THE WHOLE CLASS. Now the RHYTHM of Anger section. As before everyone takes up the chant and movement.

Find a common movement. We're all together on this, chanting, stamping, clapping, putting our feelings into our feet and bodies.

This part of the dance can be like a resolve, everyone agreeing – a positive suggestion in words and movement (e.g. "We need fresh air." "We want more bicycles"). The rhythm can be enhanced by using one group to play the rhythm on drums and shakers.

The rhythm section could be further organized by having everyone first face one direction then another.

Rhythm section

Try finishing with everyone facing FORWARD – (this would link back nicely to the beginning of the dance)

Facing forward

with ordinary, relaxed standing –
a statement in stillness.

In general terms this dance began with many angry statements, (the muttering and the partner dances) like everyone 'letting off steam', then groups form (the anger sculptures) until finally everyone joins together in one energetic and firm resolve in the unison rhythm section.

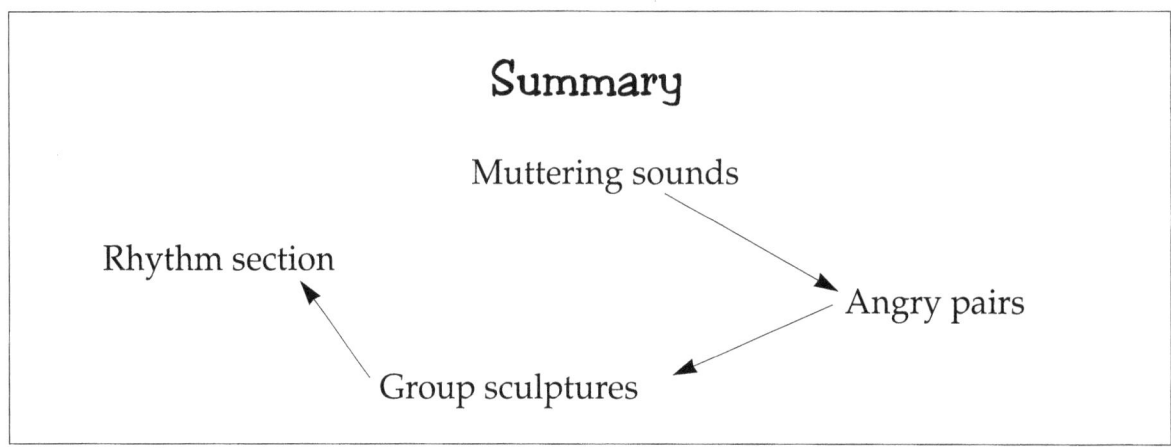

Added accompaniment could be 'newspaper slap rhythms' (newspaper folded tightly into a baton and slapped rhythmically on the floor – great fun to do).

Further activities

Write poems or paint about feelings.
Find sad songs, happy songs etc.
Make up songs of your own.

SILVER

Silver is used as a starting point for developing movement, props and music into a magical performance piece. It can be linked to a Silver Project. Consider collecting all kinds of silver things; sweet papers, tins, nails etc. and using them to make a huge silver collage or sculpture. Encourage words or poems to enlarge upon the ideas.

Visualization

Lie down on the floor on your back, close your eyes. Relax, breathe deeply with two or three deep breaths, or do this from sitting, just so long as you feel still and quiet, focused inside yourself.

Read this quietly to the children:

Imagine........s i l v e r,   shining   s i l v e r, images of silver inside your head, changing, shifting pictures, ideas of silver..........Wait for ideas to come........

> a silver river
>
> silver fruit
>
> a sword
>
> silver balls rolling along a silver road
>
> supposing everything were silver
>
> what would a silver world be like?

More...........silver aeroplanes, silver feet, silver hands,

> what would a silver world be like?

Encourage lots of suggestions.
Decide to collect some silvery things.

Here we make a silver world with :
silver balloons – you can buy silver balloons or paint them

a silver pathway – from a roll of shiny bubble wrap, cut a long
                        strip

silver hands – polythene gloves – buy on a roll from a
                chemist – painted or decorated with glitter

silver fabric – bubble wrap or silver wrapping paper or
                fabric – cut into large squares and decorated.

Now we have four types of object with which to set the scene.

You will also need a triangle, a drum, a cymbal and a woodblock or xylophone
to make accompaniment.

Making movement

1. The silver balloons

*(Using imaginary ones to begin with encourages the gentle movement quality. This
section could be a warm up.)*

Accompaniment
a silver triangle

IMAGINE you have a silver balloon, holding it very gently between your
hands. You throw it slow motion to me and I throw it softly back. It should
look as if we really are holding a balloon.

Now you can practise that idea with a partner bending and stretching,
making variations on the movement – working in tandem together:

throwing up high, or near to the ground, across your back, or.......so you
are bending and twisting and turning.

*Another preparatory idea would be to gently pass a real balloon around in a circle.
Use real silver BALLOONS or practice ones of any colour.*

The children can sit at one side and take turns to use the balloons. Comment on the skills and movement that you observe so that each group gets ideas from watching the others. Organize about five people at a time each with a balloon.

Begin to toss them lightly up, just a little way. Toss up and floating down......gently undulating.... finding your own variations.
Follow the movement of the balloon with your own body.

Then at a signal all stopping very still.............

Silver stillness holding your position and the balloon very still.

Now five other people can take over your roles with the balloons.

They can slide into your positions, beginning from the

Position you stopped in,

Like stepping into your skins.

In this way everyone can have a go.

2. A silver pathway -

moving SLOWLY

Accompaniment
A soft drumbeat

Again all the children can try this. Two groups at a time, the rest watching.

1. Travel in threes one behind the other with a good space between you. Travel very CAREFULLY and SLOWLY along it- -

Try....a follow my leader movement. Take it in turns to lead.
What silvery way of moving occurs to you along this shining, silver pathway ?
e.g. Hands leading, feet leading the movement, or elbow or back, using rolling or stretching. Develop your follow my leader movement.

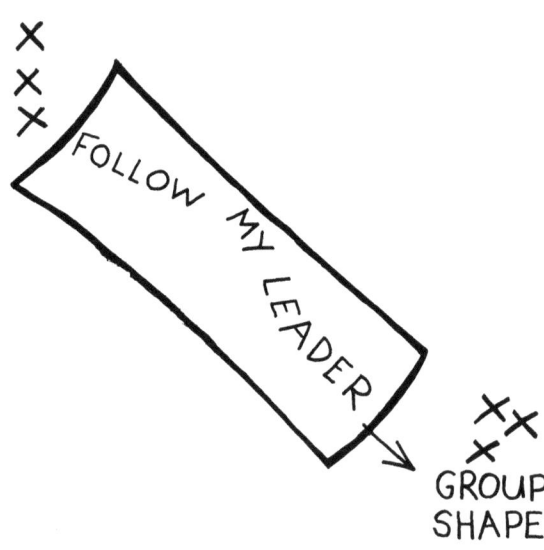

2. At the end of the pathway, make a GROUP SHAPE by fitting in to the body shape of the one preceding you. And then be ready to move one by one, in follow my leader formation, back along the pathway again.

3. Discuss what the pathway means or represents to you. Perhaps it is the pathway to the moon, or a silver river? How did you have to move? Practise your pathway movements altogether, this time not travelling on the fabric, but imagining it.

3. Silver fabric

Accompaniment
A cymbal

Practise this idea in a largish group. Each child has a square of silver fabric and works individually but aware of others nearby. Encourage movement contrasts.

This is like a

Silver wind

Filling the space.

Holding the corners

Of the fabric

Begin to move it

Gently up and down

Using your arms and

Your whole upper body

In the movement.

Make patterns and pathways in the space

Around you.

Keep your feet firmly on the ground

Fill the space above you

With the fabric.

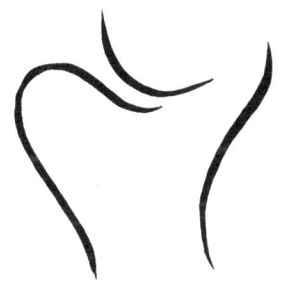

Arch your spine

Sink down then

Toss up again.

Again children can take turns to use the fabric. Perhaps half the class at a time. Or one group could use the fabric with the others echoing their movements.

4. Silver hands - everywhere

Accompaniment

a woodblock or xylophone

Introduce the idea with the children sitting down, focusing on and watching their hands, making them for example stretch, twist, turn and vibrate.

In groups of four, make silver movements with your hands, responding to each other's conversation. You can decorate and wear the gloves later.

e.g.
1. In a circle facing inwards, lift your hands altogether high in the centre, like a cluster of hands and then find two other movements before repeating the phrase.

2. Stand beside each other in a line and move your hands up and down, in and out,

this way, that way,

fast and slow like birds flying ....

silver birds.

3. Travel lightly amongst each other, weaving in and out, high and low, twisting and turning your hands in the spaces between you like making silver pathways in the space.

Once everyone has practised, select who is to be in each group.
Divide the class up into four categories - Balloons, Pathway, Fabric and Hands.

Practise now all four of these sections with and without using the actual props.
Encourage taking time to feel at home with the movements. Try out possibilities.

Putting it all together

SILVER BALLOONS accompanied by the triangle

SILVER PATHWAY accompanied by the drum

SILVER FABRIC accompanied by the cymbal

SILVER HANDS accompanied by the wood block

THE DANCE

There are so many ways to fill the space with silver, with movement and with stillness.

First of all we will decide where in the space to place all the groups and the props.

The silver pathway could bisect the space diagonally.

Details
The general idea is that the movement begins ONE group at a time, so that gradually more and more people are moving and the whole space is filled with wonderful silver images and movement, a climax of silver!

And then gradually the process is reversed, one group at a time stopping, until once more there is stillness and the silver shapes of stillness.

Each person now is very still in their chosen starting position, ready to move.

Each group begins a few phrases after the one before –

1. With the gentle sound of the triangle, the groups with the BALLOONS begin.

2. Sound of a drumbeat.......one by one the people move along the SILVER PATHWAY to the end and merge into their group shape.

Once everyone is there, they move back along the pathway again.

3. Sound of the cymbal reverberating.......the SILVER FABRIC people move.

4. Sound of wood block or xylophone......SILVER HANDS move and dart in the space

Once they have begun, each group KEEPS MOVING so for a short while all the sound and movement is happening simultaneously......Make a CLIMAX (e.g. make the accompaniment louder, the movements bigger or faster).

Then in the same order that they began, each group stops in turn, guided by the sound of their instrument.

Triangle sound ceases   (BALLOONS hold still)

Drum   (PATHWAY pauses)

Cymbal   (FABRIC is still)

Woodblock or xylophone   (HANDS stop moving)

Gradually all movement ceases as group by group comes to stillness.

As a final statement everyone whispers   "S I L V E R

```
        S
          I
            L
              V
                E
                  R
                      silver"
```

Summary

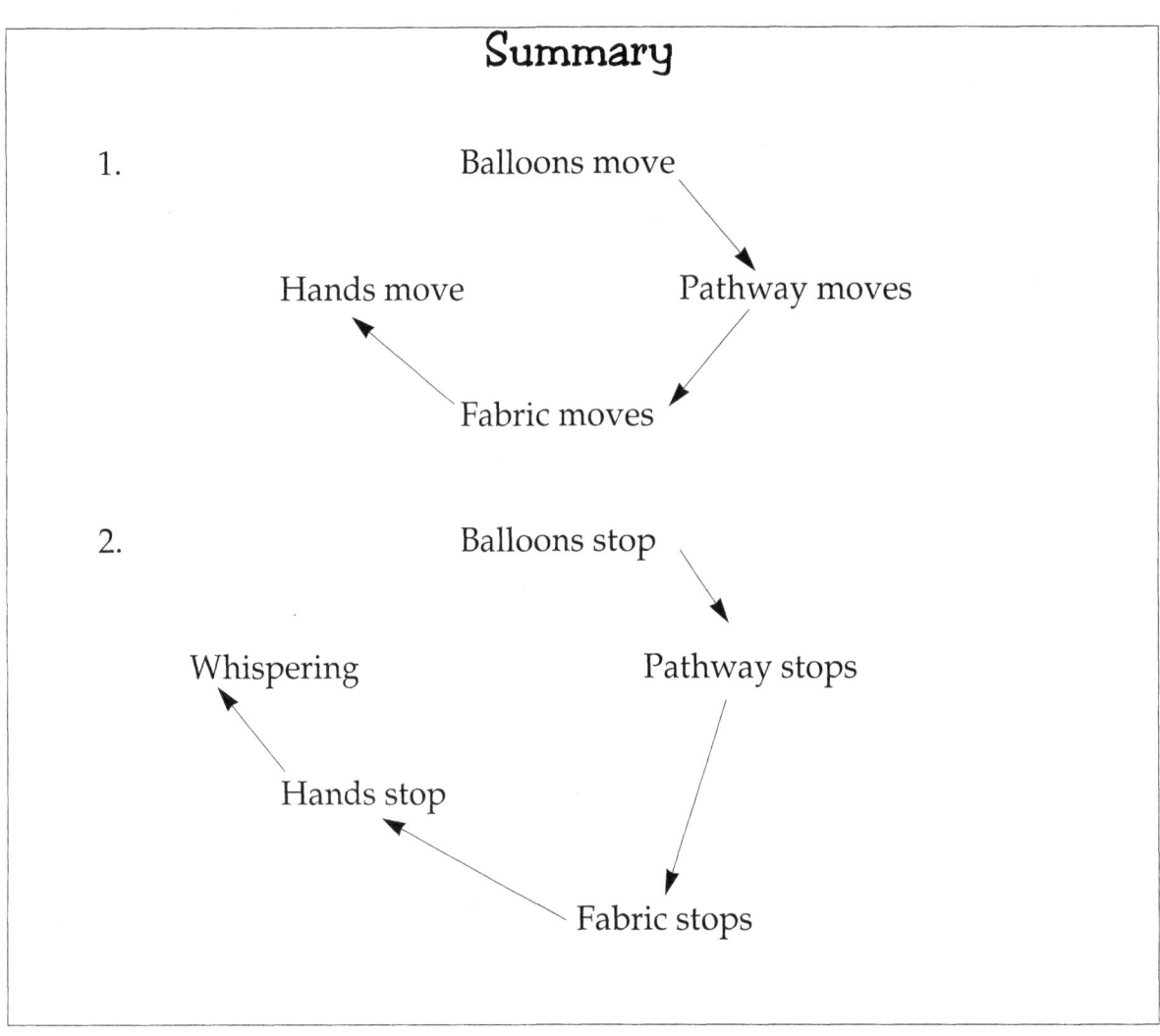

1.

Balloons move

Hands move → Pathway moves

Fabric moves

2.

Balloons stop

Whispering → Pathway stops

Hands stop

Fabric stops

Related activities

Silver collages
Silver sculpture including same materials as used in dance
Silver mining – finding out about it
Silver poems and stories
Tape recording the accompaniment.

See the NES Arnold catalogue for paint and glitter.

Endnote
First created as an outdoor community performance for the London Borough of Hounslow, involving children, young people and adults, musicians and dancers.

DANCING OUT OF DOORS

This chapter presents ideas for dancing, using nature as a source of movement and feeling. When we dance out of doors we are not so much using the landscape and the elements as becoming at one with them, identifying and responding to their inherent qualities. The focus is on the experience of nature through movement, not only the knowing about. This is a different approach from using an image from nature as a starting point for movement.

Moving with this awareness can put us in touch with our own physicality and remind us of our essential interconnectedness to nature without which the health of ourselves and the planet may suffer.

We may all have childhood memories of playing when the outdoors was a source of adventure and sometimes, of comfort, e.g. hiding in long grass, rolling down slopes or noticing the smells of country or seaside.

The opportunities for such work may arise from a walk, or in the context of an expedition or outing, where the opportunities for dancing may be part of the overall idea and rhythm of the day. Such events have sometimes been the culmination of several groups working separately and then combining their efforts in performance. On the other hand it is likely that outdoor dances will often be transitory, made in the moment and not necessarily repeated.

The following dances exemplify a method of working out of doors where the movement ideas come from direct contact with the natural environment.

GRASS DANCES

Visualization

Stand

Feel the grass

Under your

Bare feet.

Feel its

Texture

And its

Temperature

Imagine you

Breathe out through

Your heels.

Making movement

1. Begin to walk slowly, at first very slowly, taking plenty of time to savour the grass under your feet.

WALKING SLOWLY

Then a little faster, then more until you are running lightly, curving and turning across the grass, skilfully making your own pathways past and around other people, keeping your distance, keeping your running smooth. Until on a given signal:
you pause, hold your position lightly, listening, ready to choose a new direction.

Then off again, walking, into running, continually creating running patterns on the grass.

Repeat this lots of times, so you become skilful at organizing flowing ground patterns, noticing how your body adapts to the curves by leaning into the direction. Keep yourself light and up in your upper body while remaining sensitive to the ground.

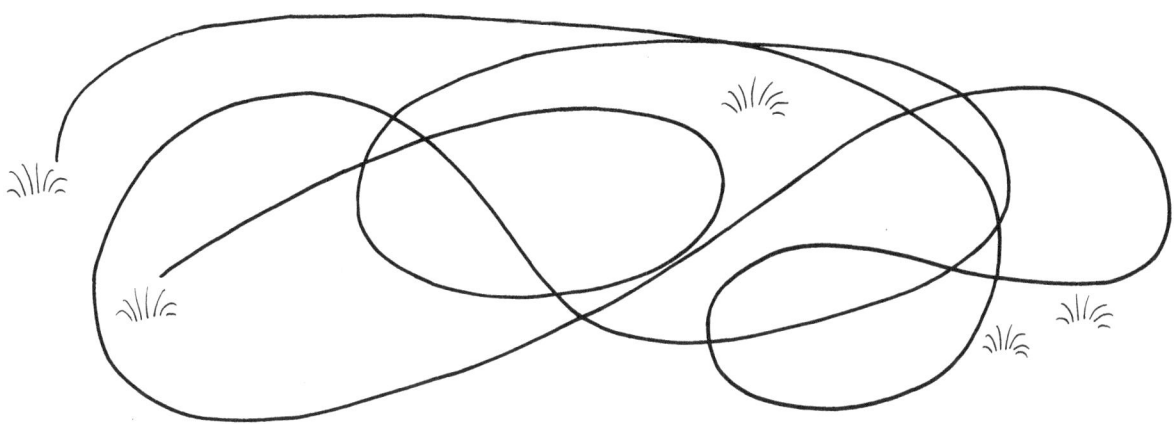

2. Now create some other grass dance movements. Try them on your own first of all and then in groups of THREE. e.g:

Touching, touching the grass

With your hands then

Leaping up towards

The sky

Four leaps high

Up, up, up

Up.

Then gently down

To touch the grass

Again.

Or

Swaying into

Spiralling down

And rolling.... rolling......

Stretched out long and narrow.

Touching the grass

With all of yourself

Then rolling up to stand and

Sway again.

Or

Follow my leader movements:

Slow stretchy walks,

Wide armed turns

Dipping up and down

Towards and away

From the grass.

Maybe you are tracking........What can you devise?

DANCING
IN
3's

Practise your idea in your groups of three.

Make it clear whether you are doing different movements, fitting in with each other or all moving in unison.

Have a beginning and an end to your idea.

Could you make some voice sounds or words to go with the movement?

THE DANCE

1. Begin in stillness. Then everyone begin walking, running, making individual curving patterns across the grass. Have lots of pauses. People could be pausing at different moments. Cover the grass with huge, sweeping grass tracks.

   Then slow down and run to JOIN THE OTHERS IN YOUR GROUP of three, into a space of stillness. Gradually everyone is still.

2. Two or three groups at a time perform their group movements. As they finish, the next groups begin (they may not necessarily finish at the same time in which case there might be some interesting overlaps.)

3. Repeat the individual running ideas again.

Then to end, at a given signal suggest everyone runs, still on curving pathways, towards the centre of the group and then continues running very CLOSE but not TOUCHING, weaving in and out, in amongst each other. Then slowly, slowly stopping...... and all slowly raising their arms in a unison movement towards the sky.

This running close is very enjoyable to do and creates a great feeling of rhythmic unity.

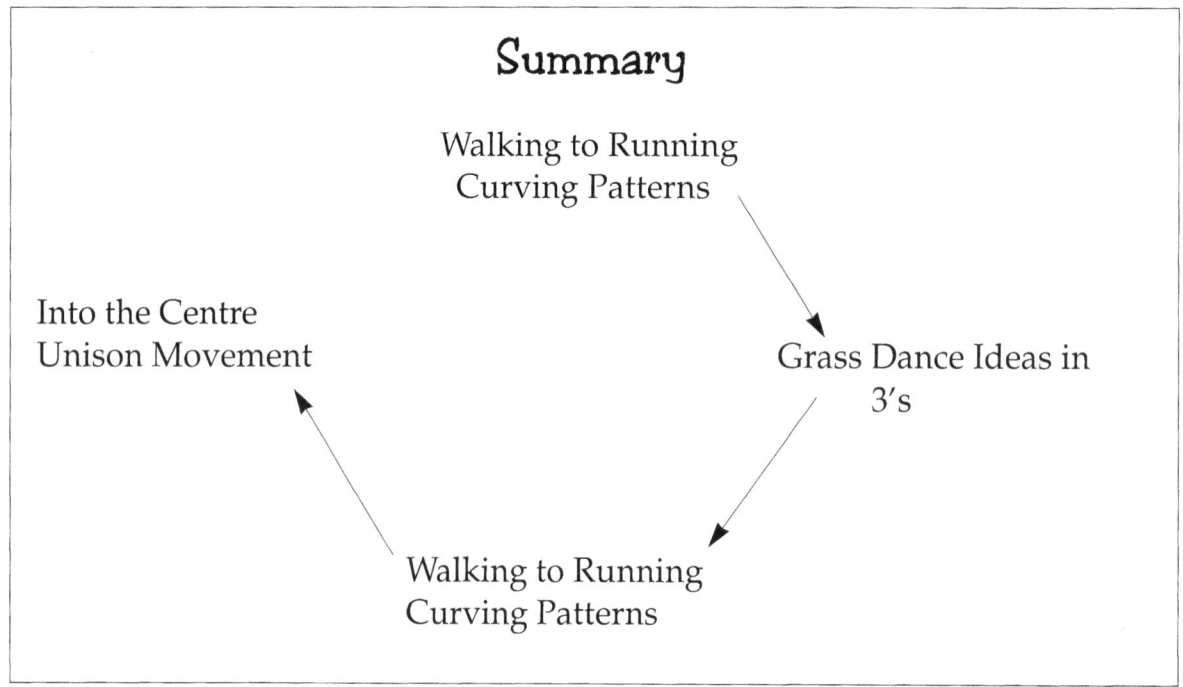

Summary

Walking to Running
Curving Patterns

Into the Centre
Unison Movement

Grass Dance Ideas in
3's

Walking to Running
Curving Patterns

Accompaniment

Out of doors, live music is best. Organize a group of drummers or recorder players for the running and perhaps encourage quietish voice sounds for the small group movement.

Additional ideas

The basic idea in this dance could also be adapted for different environments, on sand, or in a playground.

It is also possible to bring the dance indoors, by photographing or filming it and recreate the movements alongside the photographs or film.

Myths and symbols connected to Nature are to be found in all cultures. Try collecting some. (The classic 'The Golden Bough'* for adults is a useful source where movement is linked to symbolic meanings e.g. spring rituals.)

Make a COLLAGE or a MASK using natural objects – wood, grass, flowers, sand etc.
e.g.
Try collages made of sycamore seeds in a 'spinning' design
or
Leaf skeletons
or
use small pieces of wood, tiny stones, pressed flowers
or
shells, sand or seaweed.

Use paper, card or wood as a backing and glue on the natural objects.

Make MASKS based on cardboard plates devised and decorated with natural objects as above.
Use what you find in the outside environment in the countryside or in the town.

The Golden Bough A Study in Magic and Religion by J. G. Frazer (Papermac 1987)

The following sketches in words and drawings were both a plan and a record of an out of doors project for young people with disabilities, some with wheelchairs. It included creating movement, song and rhythm from the surrounding landscape.

It is presented here as a stimulus for ideas and to convey the spirit of working from Nature. Following ancient Aboriginal belief the project was called *Dancing the World into being Afresh*.

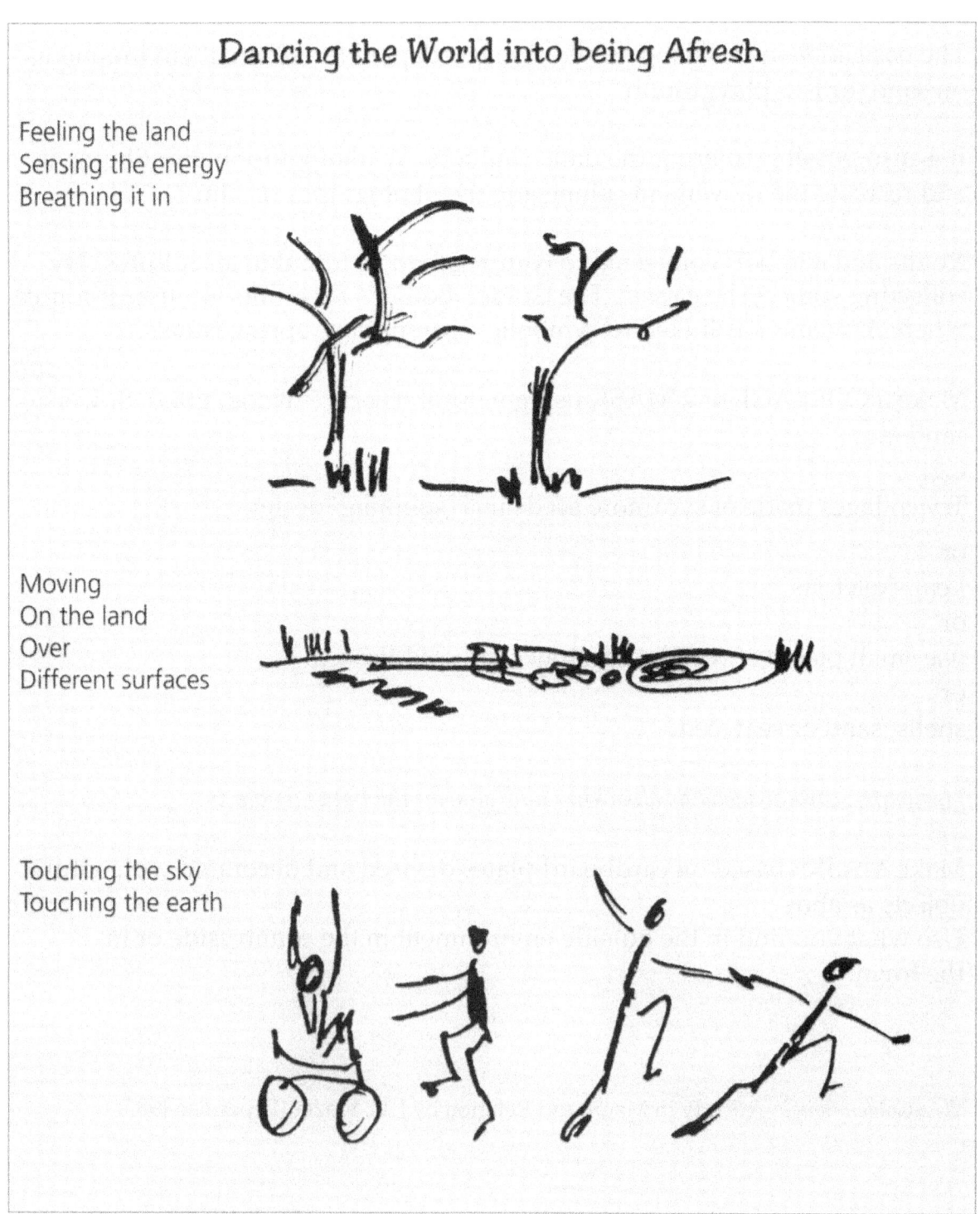

Dancing the World into being Afresh

Feeling the land
Sensing the energy
Breathing it in

Moving
On the land
Over
Different surfaces

Touching the sky
Touching the earth

Singing what you
Can see
Into a song

Finding objects
Tangible Memories

Trees
Movement and
Rhythm

Coming together

Watching and Joining

Single file

Stillness

The Healing
In Landscape

Sea
Wind Grass Sun
Rain Trees and
Air

We begin with what the land suggests to us -
Breathing, stretching, turning, running
Finding a shape, a rhythm
A movement to dance with the
Earth.

We come together and
Listen
To ourselves and to the
Land.

Nurturing awareness of
Self,
Others and
Environment
Through our bodies and movement.

Finding Joy

At the end of the day
Recollecting and remembering.

A

Goodbye
Dance

Endnote
This project took place out of doors at Holton Lee Centre, Poole Dorset

CELEBRATIONS

Incorporates ideas from ancient circle dances, creating variations of traditional steps – hops, stamps and jumps. Drawing on a Mexican background of colour and rhythm it explores images of Aztec life and includes directions for making *Pinatas*.

What do we know about MEXICO ?

High mountains ~~ tropical coastlines ~~ vivid colours ~~
Indians ~~

Aztecs ~~ Spaniards ~~ tortillas ~~ Popocatepetl ~~
festivals ~~ Tenochtitlan ~~ eagle ~~

snake ~~ cactus ~~ sacred ball game ~~pinatas ~~
circle dances

The folk dances in Mexico are often hundreds of years old, some from as far back as the Aztecs or even earlier. Many of the 'Indianos' dances are connected to particular seasons of the year and ancient spiritual beliefs. Later dances depict the everyday life of the people. Here the Mexican 'flavour' is suggested by examples of particular stepping patterns, but obviously feel free to improvise at will.

First of all we will make some circle dances; expressions of vitality and celebration, and then lead on to making Movement images from Mexican life and history.

Making movement

1. CIRCLE DANCES

Imagine

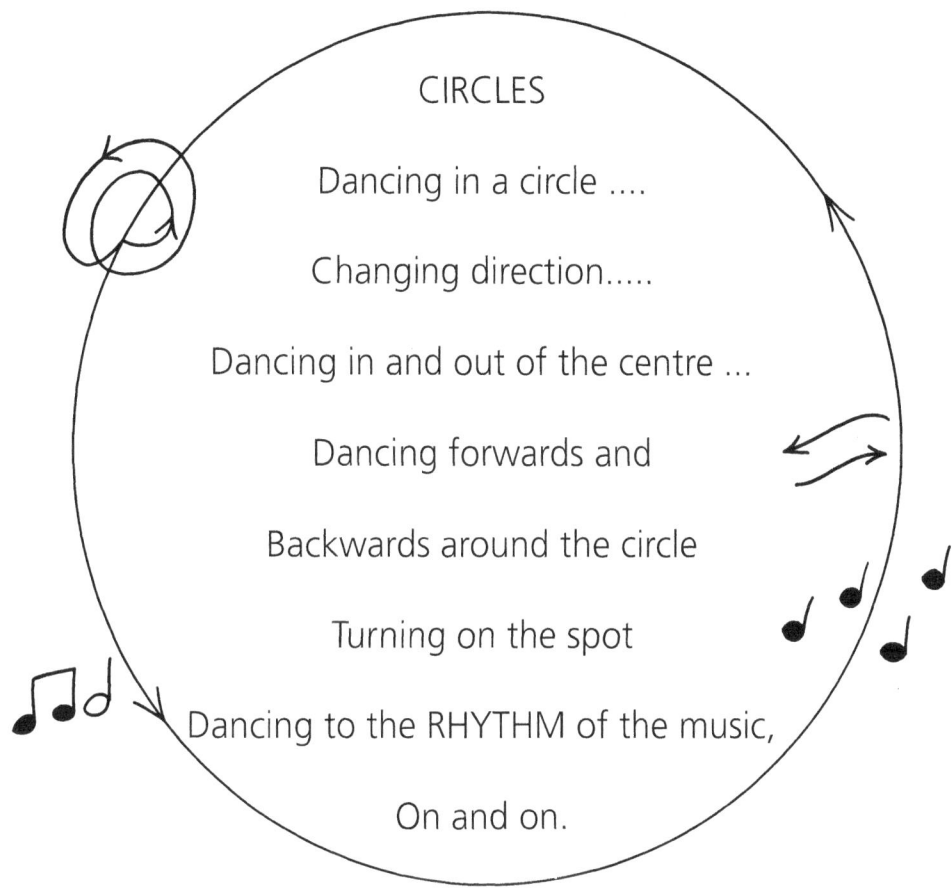

CIRCLES

Dancing in a circle ....

Changing direction.....

Dancing in and out of the centre ...

Dancing forwards and

Backwards around the circle

Turning on the spot

Dancing to the RHYTHM of the music,

On and on.

Throughout history circles have represented unity and the eternal.

Listen to the music. What sort of steps can we make to the rhythm of the music? Tap out the rhythm with your feet.

Mexican folk dances include lots of hopping, stepping and stamping and brush steps. The spine is usually kept quite upright or tilted slightly forward from the hips. The accent is down, firm and strong, with connection to the earth, not light and upward.

Find a variety of simple stepping patterns which can be repeated over and over.

These could be devised individually all about the room, or altogether in one big circle picking up from each other and trying out different ideas.

Example

These type of step patterns could be developed gradually, adding actions as children become familiar with the rhythm. Aim for simplicity and rhythmic flow. Use the children's suggestions too.

1. TRAVELLING ROUND THE CIRCLE

Walking – walking – walking – walking
stamp – stamp STEP hop
stamp – stamp STEP hop
Walking – walking – walking – walking
stamp–stamp STEP hop
stamp–stamp TURN

skip – skip – step step step JUMP
skip – skip – step step step JUMP
skip – skip – step step step JUMP
Hop – hop – hop as you turn
Hop – hop – hop as you turn

2. THEN REPEAT THIS TOWARDS AND AWAY FROM THE CENTRE OF THE CIRCLE

3. ON THE SPOT, TRY THIS AUTHENTIC MEXICAN STEP

Start with **both feet together.** Step forward onto Right heel (take your weight on it) and then immediately step back onto left foot and right foot with two little stamps on left and right. Repeat with the left heel (weight on right foot) Now FAST!

(R) Heel – step step
(L) Heel – step step
(R) Heel – step step
(L) Heel – step step

(R) Heel – step step
(L) Heel – step step
Half – a – turn

Enjoy your rhythms. Practise them over and over until they feel a part of you.

To practise, half the class could stand in a circle, clapping and stamping the rhythm, with the other half of the class inside the circle, practising the steps.
Practise with and without the music.
Then divide the class into manageable circles so each works out its own variation.

A Conchero Dance Group at Amecameca, Mexico

2. MAKING GROUP IMAGES OR PICTURES

Remember all the images of Mexico that you thought of earlier:

High mountains – tropical coastlines – vivid colours –

Indians – Aztecs – Spaniards –

tortillas – Popocatepetl – festivals –

Tenochtitlan – eagle – snake – cactus –

sacred ball game – pinatas etc.

Collect photographs and information about these, to give you ideas for your group.

How would you make a group shape based on one of these?

Choose some images and build group 'pictures' based on the above, or any other images of Aztec life.

A group picture is built up by each person in turn moving from the edge of the circle into the centre to build up a still group shape that represents an idea.
E.g "What do you look like as ......?"

Each in turn moves into the centre and then holds their chosen position very still.
E.g. The first child moves into the centre and crouches low with arms outspread. The second child joins and stretches high above the first child.

It is important to take some time to really imagine the scene and to imagine your part in it. This prepares you for movement and prevents the 'knee jerk' reaction where everyone tends to copy everyone else.

Group pictures are fun to do. Play around with a variety of ideas. Encourage the children's inventiveness, in fitting in with each other's body shapes and ideas.

Here are three ideas for group pictures.

(i). The Snake, Eagle and Cactus

Following the dictates of their high priest, the Aztec city of Tenochtitlan (which is Mexico City today) was built in the place where an EAGLE was seen eating a SNAKE on a CACTUS bush.
This scene is depicted on the Mexican national flag.

To make the Snake, Eagle and Cactus picture, begin in your circle., e.g.
a) Make a circle of eight children. Number yourselves 1 to 8. Then.....

b) .....children **1** to **4** move one by one into the centre of the circle to form
      a prickly cactus shape.
Each fits into the shape of the one before.

5 & **6** move ditto to form an eagle shape.

7 & **8** move to form the snake shape.

Make the movement into the centre fit the image, e.g. travelling with
sharp, jerky movements of fingers, elbows, knees for the cactus.
Practise this slowly at first.
(Call out "number 1 move, 2 move, 3 move" etc.) See the diagram below

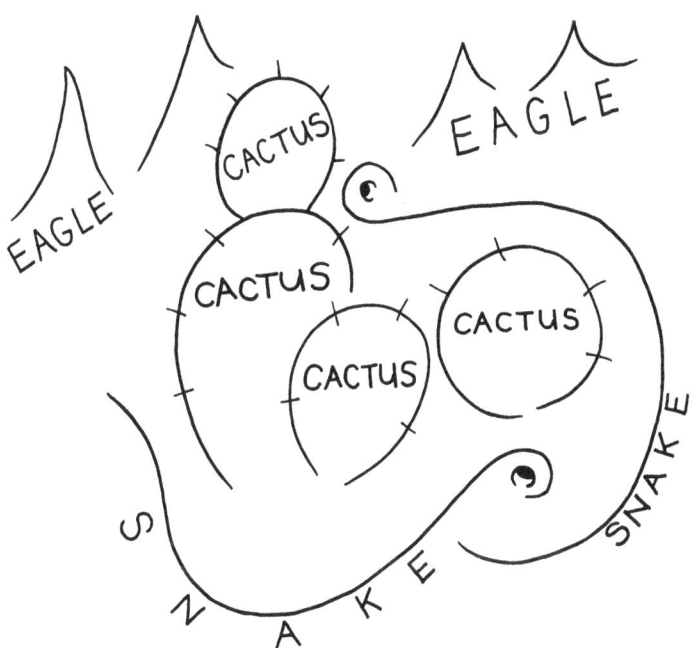

Freeze the picture for several moments and then move in character back to
your place in the circle again.

*It is useful to literally demonstrate this format first with one group of children. The
essence is to move and be still – move and be still.*

*To develop the idea a little further the 'picture' could move briefly, the body shapes
changing within it. e.g. The cactus grows higher, wider and lower over a count of one,
two, three.*

Alternatively you might prefer to make three separate groups – eagle, cactus and
snake.

(ii). A Battle Scene

Diego Rivera, the famous Mexican artist, painted huge WALL PAINTINGS depicting scenes from Mexican history, sometimes showing BATTLE scene between Cortes and the Aztecs with their leader Montezuma.

Make a picture of a battle scene with:

Fierce advancing body shapes

Ducking, avoiding

Crumpling

Leaping

Running away

Here the shapes would be based on action and reaction to each other.
E.g. One leaps high and lands in a fierce position. The other ducks low in a protective body shape, or, 'Freezing' the action of one chasing the other.
Focus too on how you feel in that shape – frightened, angry, sad.
The movement could be a springboard for real empathy with the people at that time.

(iii). Group Mountains

Make yourselves into famous GROUP MOUNTAINS -

named Popocatepetl and Ixtaccihuatl (the Mountain of Fire and the White Princess)

Divide the children into groups. Each group makes a mountain shape. As in the 'Snake, Eagle and Cactus' example, move one by one into the centre of the circle – move and hold your position – building up the shape of the mountain: a people mountain.

Be like rocks – make yourselves into two group shapes

Start with low, lying down rocks,

Then higher, kneeling ones,

Then half standing

To
Standing ones.

And finally

Clouds

The

To

Reaching

Up ones

Stretching

Read about the legend of the two sacred mountains and look at paintings and drawings of the Aztec period for more ideas for movement image.

Practise some SPANISH PHRASES for calling out at the beginning of the dance.

Put a noisy jumble of these on tape!

Hola (Hello) or Adios   (Goodbye)

¿Como estas?   (How are you?)

Muy bien   (Very well)

"Hola!"

THE DANCE

Introduction

Play the tape recorded jumble of Spanish!

Everyone enters the space making their way into their circles. As they do this they greet each other:

HOLA ..... ADIOS etc.

1. Everyone stands ready in their circles. The CIRCLE DANCES begin with the music. After a given amount the music pauses and each circle is still.

2. Make the GROUP PICTURES in the centre of the circles.

1. and 2. might be alternated several times. The music can be paused or faded down and up again for the pictures.

3. Devise an ENDING - perhaps finishing in the circle with the whole class doing the same, everyone becoming part of one whole class picture. For example:

Hola!

We all raise our arms into the air

Celebrating Mexico,

Hola!

Or we make a picture of us all

Eating Mexican CHOCOLATE -

Yummmee.

In Aztec belief the cocoa seeds were considered of divine origin and only very important people were allowed the 'cacao' drink.

Summary

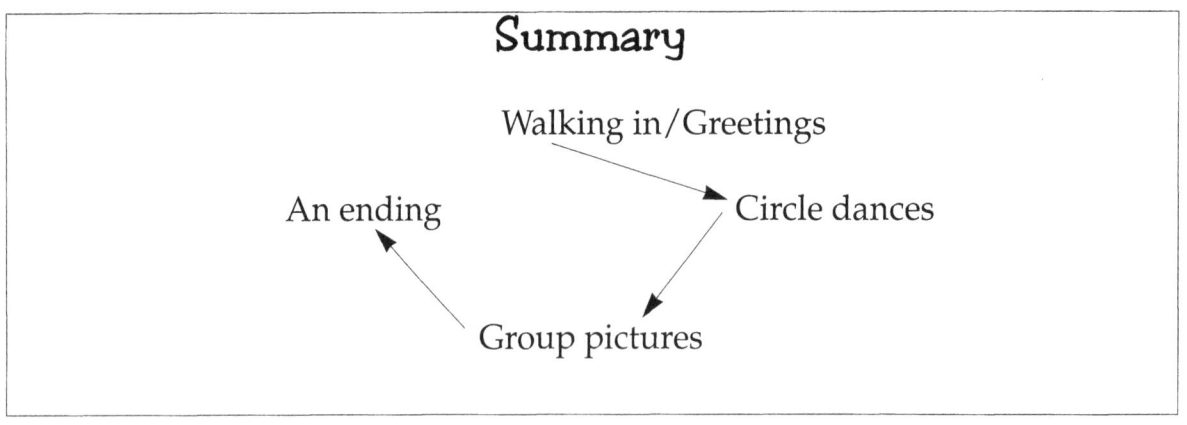

Walking in/Greetings

An ending   Circle dances

Group pictures

Music

From *Mexico Fiestas of Chiapas and Oaxaca* (compact disc Explorer Series '76)

Costumes

Base each circle on a different colour, reflecting the vivid colours of Mexico; bright red, yellow, deep blue etc.

Dye T shirts or use fabric paint to make Mexican-type designs, as below.

Make long plaits of coloured wool and then plait them into belts to tie around the waist.

Make a big PINATA

Put papier mâché over a large inflated balloon. Stick FOUR cardboard horns onto it. Cover and decorate it with fringes of coloured crêpe paper.

When it is dry, burst the balloon and fill the space inside with sweets. In Mexico the piñata is hung from the ceiling and children are blindfolded and in turn given an opportunity to break the piñata with a stick.

When it is broken, all the sweets tumble out and everyone shares them. These piñatas are produced in all shapes and sizes for celebrations. They might be part of your dance scenario.

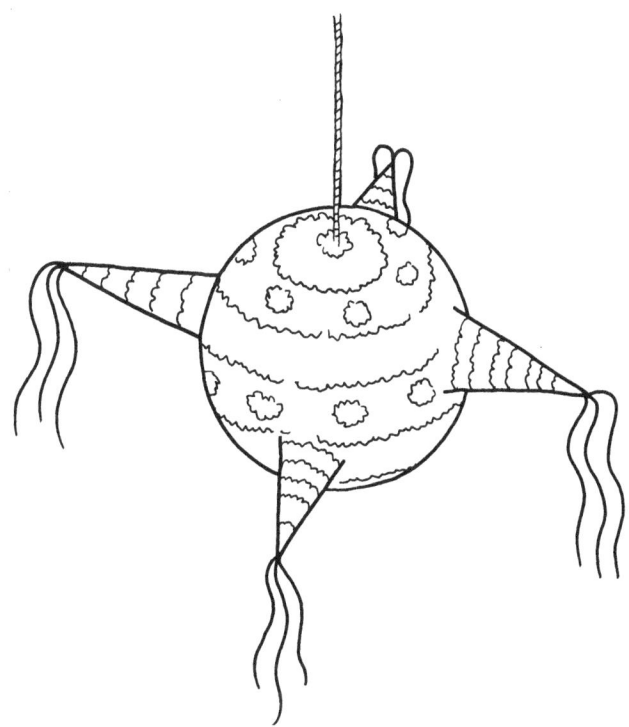

Also make brightly painted clay animals and birds and seed necklaces, which are all deeply rooted in Mexican tradition from very ancient times.

The dance ideas in this chapter could also be used in relationship to other countries, taking the music and the cultural background as starting points.

See *Arts and Crafts of Mexico* by Chloe Sayer (Thames and Hudson)

Endnote
Celebrations is dedicated to Antonia Guerrero, leader of a Conchero Dance Group, with which I was privileged to perform. (Conchero Dance uses ancient forms going right back to pre-Aztec times.)

Connections to the National Curriculum

Imaginary Dances supports the National Curriculum and in fact goes beyond its dictates. The focus in this book is on creating dances and defining the different aspects within that process.

The skills involved are in: creativity
> formulating and communicating ideas
> self management and
> creating and maintaining relationships.

Reflect on making dance movement part of school life. Weave it into the curriculum in ways suggested and also for celebrations – to mark an occasion – or even the beginning and ending of the working day.

Dance Key Stage 1

Show control and co-ordination, through the basic actions of travelling, jumping, turning, gesture and stillness.

The above are both implicit and explicit and encouraged throughout the book by means of a wide variety of language and examples.

Perform simple rhythmic patterns using movement expressively to explore moods and feelings in response to stimuli including music

Rhythmic patterns of movement are included throughout.

Rhythmic response is encouraged throughout including suggestions for percussion, music, voice and creative sound accompaniments.

Expressive movement from a range of stimuli is central to the book.

Dance Key Stage 2

Compose and combine basic actions through the use of varying shape, size, direction, level, speed, tension and continuity.

These are among the basic tenets for composition in each dance and can be varied at will.

Perform dances from different places and times.

Universal stepping patterns are to be found in many chapters.

'Celebrations' chapter connects to this section.

Express feelings, moods and ideas in movement, responding to stimuli including music.

Feelings, moods and ideas are starting points for movement throughout **Imaginary Dances.**

Dance Key Stage 3

The contents of the book are applicable to Key Stage 3 in the context of using pupils' observation and response relative to their age and ability to any of the earlier Key Stage requirements.

The movement content of the book provides more than the National Curriculum requirements but the Key Stage 1 and 2 criteria form a useful checklist, remembering the importance of observation and repetition in development of skills.

Make a note beside each chapter of what *you* yourself have particularly observed and encouraged with your class e.g. the ability to make clear changes of direction.

In general when you evaluate the work look for the degree and development of:

a) concentration and absorption.

b) whole body participation in the movement.

c) increasing awareness and control of action, and the time-weight-space and relationship aspects of the movement.

d) increasing clarity in response to mood, image, music or character.

The increasing clarity of the movement and the expressive potential are inseparable.

The National Curriculum Attainment Targets for the end of Key Stage descriptions are also applicable.

Cross-curricular activities

Art= (A), History = (H), Music = (M), Language = (L)

CHAPTERS

Animals	Creating accompaniment with words (M) Fabric painting (A)
Myself	Creating body maps (A & L) Creative writing (L) Anatomy and physiology
Story in Movement	Creating accompaniment (L & M)
Wheels	Creating accompaniment, a collage of sounds (M) Researching wheels (H) Creating a wheel collage or sculpture (A)
Dreams	Face painting (A)
Feelings	Poems and paintings (L& A) Songs (M)
Silver	Decorating props (A) Collages (A) Sculpture (A) Mining – research (H) Creative writing (L) Tape recording accompaniment (M)
Dancing Out of Doors	Collecting nature myths and symbols (L) Mask making from natural materials (A)
Celebrations	Researching Aztec culture/history (H) Making a *pinata* (A) Using dye, fabric paint and wool to create costumes. (A)

Link the above with N.C. requirements in:
ART see *Investigating and Making*, Key Stage 1 and 2
MUSIC *Performing and Composing* Key Stage 1 and 2
HISTORY – Key Stage 2

In addition *spoken* language may be enriched alongside *movement* language and vice versa.

SOURCES OF INFORMATION

National Resource Centre for Dance
The University of Surrey
Guildford
Surrey GU2 5XH

Foundation for Community Dance
13–15 Belvoir Street
Leicester LE1 6SL
Tel. 0116 275 5057

Arts Council of Great Britain
14 Great Peter Street
London,
SW1P 3NG
Tel 0171 333 0100
Yellow & blue leaflets list support organizations and dance education officers in main dance companies.
Community Dance - a progress report.
Dance Pack - information about dance education undertaken by dance companies.

Mexico Lore
28 Warrimer Gardens
London SW11 4EB
for information on Mexican culture

Rosa Shreeves
24 Strand on the Green
London W4 3PH
workshops, dance projects, therapy

About the Author

Rosa Shreeves is a Dance Artist, Teacher and Therapist.

She has performed and taught extensively in schools and colleges, arts centres and community settings and has extensive experience in choreography as a solo artist, with her own company and others. She is also a registered Integrative Arts Therapist.

Her writing includes the books *Children Dancing*, *Moves*, (co-author), radio scripts on dance for children and a variety of articles and poetry. She has spent time in Mexico and has a particular interest in Mexican dance and culture.

She works freelance for organizations in the UK and abroad, notably with dance and environmental projects and has a private practice in London for movement and dance therapy and massage.

Lightning Source UK Ltd.
Milton Keynes UK
UKOW07f1921070217

293859UK00011B/447/P